Praise for G

About His Writing:

AWARDS:

The Gate of Beautiful: Stories, Songs, and Reflections on Christian Life THE NATIONAL BEST BOOK AWARDS 2009 Finalist, USA Book News "EVVY" Book Awards 2010, First place: Religion.

REVIEWS:

"As I read though the chapters of *The Shepherd's Watch*, two things jump out at me. First, Jerry loves Jesus and second, Jesus's love for "even the least of these" is reflected through Jerry's life in his daily encounters with the people the Lord brings along his path."
—Reverend Dr. Kenneth W. Smith
Pastor, First Baptist Church of Shelton

"There are many ways people express themselves, and author Gerald Rasmussen taps into a wealth of them. *The Gate of Beautiful: Stories, Songs, and Reflections on Christian Life* is a collection of creative exercises. Christian in focus, Rasmussen's songs, stories, and essays provide much insight into man's faith, which is sure to give readers much to think about. *The Gate of the Beautiful* is quite a pick for Christian readers, highly recommended."
Midwest Book Review
(Oregon, WI USA)

"Jerry Rasmussen is one of those rare writers who makes it look deceptively easy to express wisdom, employing wit, homilies, and poignancy to show the deeper values that lie within the everyday comedies and tragedies of life. His writing is lively, engaging, and utterly delightful."

Miriam Hospodar
Author of *Heaven's Banquet*

ABOUT HIS SONGS:
"Your music was sincere and reached down into the mind and soul to minister and uplift our spirits. You focused on the abounding grace of God through Jesus Christ with every song."

—Rev. John Hagin
First Baptist Church, Ansonia, CT

"This album (*The Secret Life of Jerry Rasmussen*) is like a visit with an old friend, so pull up a chair."

—Tom Paxton
Folk recording artist

"A songwriter of rare warmth and humor, a gentle realist with a fine and wiley wit."

—Gordon Bok
Folk recording artist

"Jerry brings an intimate, homey sort of perspective to his youth and childhood in the Midwest, describing through his songs the same sort of environment that Garrison Keillor eulogized in the *Newses*."

—Clyde Tynsdale
Woods Hole Music Society

"Rasmussen is a great songwriter. Period."
—Gene Petit, John Henry's Hammer, Worcester, MA

the SHEPHERD'S WATCH

the SHEPHERD'S WATCH

Stories and Songs
OF FAITH

GERALD RASMUSSEN

© 2015 by Gerald Rasmussen. All rights reserved.

Published by Redemption Press, PO Box 427, Enumclaw, WA 98022 Toll Free (844) 2REDEEM (273-3336)

Redemption Press is honored to present this title in partnership with the author. The views expressed or implied in this work are those of the author. Redemption Press provides our imprint seal representing design excellence, creative content and high quality production.

No part of this publication may be reproduced, stored in a retrieval system, or transmitted in any way by any means—electronic, mechanical, photocopy, recording, or otherwise—without the prior permission of the copyright holder, except as provided by USA copyright law.

All Scripture, unless otherwise noted, is taken from the King James Version of the Holy Bible.

Verses marked NIV are taken from the *Holy Bible, New International Version*©. *NIV*©. Copyright© 1973, 1978, 1984 by International Bible Society. Used by permission of Zondervan.

ISBN 13: 978-1-63232-979-0 (Print)
    978-1-63232-980-6 (ePub)
    978-1-63232-981-3 (Mobi)

Library of Congress Catalog Card Number: 2014956931

DEDICATION

For the Shepherd

CONTENTS

Introduction xi

The Least of My Brethren 13
A Tight Spot 17
Two Joes 23
Hamburger Heaven 31
The Shepherd's Watch. 37
A Rose Remembered 43
T-Shirt Testimony 47
Jesus Loves Red Sox Ice Cream?. 51
Where Two or Three Are Gathered. 55
The Measure of Man 61
Bob-Bob-Bob, Bob-Bobra Ann. 69
I Won't Complain 75
His Eye Is on the Sparrow. 79
Meology. 85
Cutouts 89
The Eleventh Commandment. 95
A Ram in the Bush. 101

A Hoof Note	109
Speechless	111
Proud Poppas	115
A Pomegranate in a Pear Tree	119
Have Smile, Will Travel	123
Life in the Slow Lane	127
Man Kind	131
"'Twas the Night before Christmas"	137
The Graciousness of Strangers	141
Elizabeth Cotton's Banjo	147
The Impossible Just Takes Longer	151
Khristie, Brian, and St. Luke	159
The Gospel in Black and White	165
Dancing on the Toes of His Shoes	171
The Shepherd's Watch: The Song	177
Jerry's Music	179
Endnotes	181

INTRODUCTION

The Bible is full of wonderful stories. The first line of Genesis sets the tone: "In the beginning, God created Heaven and earth." It could have as easily started out, Once upon a time, God created Heaven and earth. Long before there was a Bible, when few people could read, God's story was kept alive by storytellers. The best of all the storytellers in the Bible was Jesus.

How I wish I could have been there to hear him tell his tales:

> *Those gospel nights, and the tales he told*
> *Could warm the heart, and touch the soul*
> *Oh what I'd give. It'd be my heart's delight*
> *To hear him tell those tales he told,*
> *those gospel nights*
>   *Gospel Nights* – words and music by Jerry Rasmussen

In the Bible, the tales Christ told are called parables. Parables are stories with a punch line. Christ used parables to teach important issues of faith. Like all good storytellers, Christ used vivid imagery. His stories were about ordinary people, like fishermen, farmers, sowers, and reapers. He told his stories early in the morning on the shores of Galilee, or late at night around a glowing campfire. If he were here today, you'd probably find him in a Walmart parking lot, or at the railroad station, talking to the morning commuters.

My family has a history of storytelling. My father had the knack of taking a simple experience and embellishing it through time, until it was as burnished as a brass knob. He passed that gift on to me. Over the years, I've told my stories in songs and letters. Letters are a good form of storytelling. That's what the epistles were.

The stories in this book are all true. They may have been embellished a little along the way, but the punch line still tells the tale. As I've written them down, I've gone back to the stories in the Bible, as they have often been my inspiration. Nothing is new under the sun.

THE LEAST OF MY BRETHREN

It was the catchphrase for the movie The Sixth Sense: *"I see dead people." If a Christian aspires to a sixth sense, it should be to see Christ in others. That's not nearly as easy as it may seem. Seeing Christ in Mother Theresa or the pastor of your church is one thing. Seeing him in the people you pass on the street every day is another.*

> *You pass on the street with no recognition*
> *Lost in your thoughts, you've a life of your own*
> *And if she is troubled, she keeps it well hidden*
> *She learned long ago, you must bear it alone*
>
> CHORUS:
>
> *So God bless those who find mercy in sleep*
> *All those who sow, who never will reap*
> *All those who search, and never find peace*
> *May they find rest tonight*[1]

It isn't just other people who have eyes but do not see. If Christ were standing on the corner, we could walk right by him without even noticing.

*If Jesus should come back, just for a day
And preach on that corner to all who pass by
Who'd stop and listen, and who'd walk away
And turn from salvation, and never know why?*[2]

Christ made it clear that we are to treat others as we would treat him: "Verily I say unto you, Inasmuch as ye have done it unto one of the least of these my brethren, ye have done it unto me" (Matthew 25:40).

Jesus responded with compassion to those who were in need, without precondition or judgment. He helped those who were ostracized by society, regardless of the reason for their need, or the state of their soul. How can we do less?

The day was bone-chilling cold. Looking out the front room window, the early winter sun promised a warmth it couldn't deliver. When I stepped through the doorway onto the porch, the bitter north wind hit me, causing me to involuntarily hunch my shoulders and stuff my hands deep into my pockets. It was no day to be outside.

With a turn of the key my car reluctantly started, and a blast of cold air came through the vents. I was on my way to a doctor's appointment, and I knew it would take most of the drive for the car to get warm. As I neared the office, I passed a cemetery and noticed a man walking along the side of the road pushing a supermarket shopping cart. He was all bundled up against the cold with a long jacket and a scarf tied over the top of the cap on his head. Looking over at him, all I could see of his face were a scruffy beard and long tufts of gray hair sticking out over his jacket collar. The cart was festooned with plastic shopping bags tied to the sides that flapped emptily in the wind that was cutting across the cemetery. From what I could see, the cart appeared to be empty. It looked like the man had been out searching for discarded cans along the side of the road hoping to collect enough to buy a modest breakfast with the five-cent deposits. Pickings had been slim. Maybe no one wanted to roll down their window on such a cold day to throw away their can.

I could see that he was having difficulty walking. He was using the shopping cart as a walker to support his weight. He walked hesitantly, taking small steps with one hip hiked up, carefully lifting one leg that seemed to be partially paralyzed. He was making slow progress and had to stop every few steps to catch his breath. As I was driving by him, I felt a powerful urge to go back and give him something to help make his day at least a little easier. I pulled over to the side of the road and turned my car around, heading back to where he was struggling along. He'd barely traveled ten feet.

When I approached him, he was standing on the other side of the shopping cart. I called out to him, "Excuse me," and he turned awkwardly to face me. I had expected to see an old man because his beard and hair were gray. His face was wind-bitten red and still youthful, but it was his eyes that drew me in. "I just wanted to give you this," I said, and handed him the folded ten-dollar bill I'd taken from my billfold. He took the bill from my hand and then reached his arm out to me as if he wanted to take my arm. I laid my hand gently on his arm and looked deep into his eyes. For a moment I was completely transfixed. I was overcome with the gratitude that I saw in his eyes and everything else around me faded away. He didn't speak a word, but his eyes spoke eloquently. I smiled at him and said, "Merry Christmas!" and a warm smile of appreciation spread over his face. As I walked back to the car, I realized that I was breathing shallowly, trying not to disturb the quiet peace that filled my heart.

Now I struggle to recapture the mystery of that moment. I can no longer remember the details of how the man looked, except for his eyes. It seemed like I was looking into Christ's eyes.

A TIGHT SPOT

There's no spot so tight God can't get you out of it. Look what he did for Shadrach, Meshach, and Abednego. (Or as my old friend Art Thieme liked to call them: Shadrach, Meshach and to bed you go.) Old King Nebuchadnezzar was getting hot under the collar because Shadrach, Meshach, and Abednego would not worship the golden idols. The punishment for refusing to worship the idols was death.

> *And whoso falleth not down and worshippeth, that he should be cast into the midst of a burning fiery furnace.... Then Nebuchadnezzar in his rage and fury commanded to bring Shadrach, Meshach, and Abednego, Then they brought these men before the king. Nebuchadnezzar spake and said unto them, is it true O Shadrach, Meshach, and Abednego do not ye serve my gods, nor worship the golden image which I have set up?*
> (Daniel 3:11, 13–14)

Shadrach, Meshach, and Abednego discussed among themselves what they should do. They knew if they refused to worship the golden idol, they would be cast into the furnace. With all courage, they spoke to Nebuchadnezzar.

> *If it be so, our God whom we serve is able to deliver us from the burning fiery furnace, and he will deliver us out of thy hand, O king.*

But if not, be it known unto thee, O king, that we will not serve thy gods, nor worship the golden image which thou hast set up.
(Daniel 3:17–18)

Everybody knows how that turned out. When Shadrach, Meshach, and Abednego walked out of the furnace, they were not alone.

Lo, I see four men loose, walking in the midst of the fire, and they have no hurt; and the form of the fourth is like the Son of God.
(Daniel 3:25)

As the old song says: "God will take care of you." Thank God I've never been caught in a fiery furnace. But there was a time when God rescued me from a tight spot, with an assist from Alfred Hitchcock.

I was halfway up the ladder when I heard George calling me. "Need any help?" he asked. That was George. He was always ready to help. "Thanks, George, but Ruth is right here and if I need someone to hold the ladder, she can help me."

When I got to the top of the ladder to check the damage to the roof flashing caused by the wind, I noticed that George had disappeared inside his house and reappeared wearing a coat and hat. I wasn't surprised. When my wife and I were looking for a house to buy, we prayed the Lord would give us good neighbors, and he outdid himself with George.

By the time George walked around the corner and appeared in our yard, I'd decided that it was too risky trying to repair the flashing while standing on the ladder. So, I hauled the ladder around to the deck in back of the house, propped it against the edge of the roof, and climbed up. When I got to the peak of the roof, I lay down on my stomach and looked over the edge to see the damage. I could see that two or three nails were all I needed in order to tack down the flashing. All the while George was looking up at me, calling out advice and encouragement.

"Need any nails?" he asked. I had plenty of nails in the garage, but none of them were galvanized. Regular nails would rust and stain the flashing. "I've got some galvanized nails in the garage. Just give me a minute and I'll get some for you."

A Tight Spot

Before I knew it, George had headed off around the corner and over to his garage. By the time he got back to his house, I was back down on the deck, and when he came over to the hedge that separates our property, I walked over and took a few nails out of the box. "Thanks, George," I said. "These are exactly what I need and I know I don't have any like them." I could see George was happy to help. Just in case I needed him, he made the trek around the corner one more time.

When I was done and had put the ladder away, I was standing there talking with him when George asked, "Have you turned off your outside water faucets yet?"

"I've got to tell you a funny story about that, George," I answered.

Back when we bought our house six years ago and winter was settling in, I set out to turn off the outside faucets. I knew from experience that if you didn't turn the water line off from inside the house, you risked having the lines freeze. I didn't want an indoor swimming pool in the basement, so I went down to find the water shutoffs.

Sometime after our house was built fifty some years ago, the owner constructed a secondary inner wall to finish the basement. While it made the basement look better, the inner wall created a lot of problems. The wall was framed in with two-by-four studs with barely a foot of space between the inner wall and the foundation. The main water shutoff was behind a ragged section of plasterboard that had been cut out between the studs. If you needed to turn off all the water in the house in case of an emergency, it was simply a matter of pulling out the ratty-looking section of plasterboard, reaching into the hole between the studs, and turning off the main water valve. That was the only thing that was simple.

Armed with a flashlight, I removed the section of plasterboard and peered in looking for a shutoff valve for the outside faucet. I was greeted with a maze of pipes and valves stretching ten feet back between the walls. Looking in through the hole, it was hard to figure out where the lines went and which shutoff valves might go to the outside faucet, so I gulped and tried squeezing in between the studs and the foundation. Not only was the fit distressingly tight, I had to climb up and over some of the pipes to work my way back to the shutoff valves. I finally managed to squeeze far enough in to reach over and turn off the valves, but when I tried to reverse course to get back out, I was firmly wedged between a stud and the foundation, tangled in a mess of pipes. The first image that came to mind was from the movie *Canterbury Ghost* with Charles Laughton. I'd seen that movie when I was a child and it scared the hell out of me. Laughton was tied up against a wall and slowly the opening was closed up, laying a brick at a time until finally you couldn't see his face any more. The thought of being sealed in behind a wall terrified me and I never forgot it. And then I thought of Winnie the Pooh. He'd gotten himself into a tight spot, too and his friend Rabbit told him that he'd just have to stay there without eating until he lost enough weight to get out. Some friend! I know that George would never do that.

By then, it was almost supper time. My wife, Ruth, was upstairs, but I knew she was at the other end of the house and she'd never hear me if I started yelping. I finally knew what people meant when they talked about someone who is stuck between a rock and a hard place. I was firmly wedged between a two-by-four stud and a concrete block foundation. When I finally calmed down and started breathing normally, I deflated a little. I'd been like a blowfish, all puffed up with anxiety, holding my breath. Slowly, I sucked my stomach in as hard as I could and tried to wiggle by the two-by-four. There was only one stud between me and the opening in the wall. I just had to shrink myself enough to get my stomach past the two-by-four. Why had I eaten all those doughnuts?

After much huffing and puffing, and then holding my breath between puffs, I finally squeezed by the stud with a loud "pop." Or at least that's what it felt like. When I stepped through the hole in the wallboard, I leaned against the clothes dryer and gave a sigh of relief. After I caught my breath, I headed up the basement stairs and went out the back door to check to see if I'd turned the right shutoff valves. To my consternation, the water spurted out through the faucet with disarming force. I don't know what the valves were I shut off, but they weren't for the outside faucets.

As I headed back down the basement stairway, with the jagged opening in the wallboard staring me in the face, all I could think of was that I'd have to crawl back between that stud and the foundation to turn the valves back on. I was overcome with anxiety and I could feel myself expanding in panic, just looking back between the wall and the foundation. And then I remembered Alfred Hitchcock. At the beginning of each of his TV shows, the screen would have a profile of Alfred, with his large protruding stomach. When he walked toward the center of the television screen, his shadow fit perfectly with the profile. If it worked for Alfred, why not for me?

Without hesitation, I disappeared into the garage and found my saber saw. Standing in the opening in the wallboard, I eyed up my stomach and the stud and with a ballpoint pen drew a profile of my stomach—just like Alfred. It only took a minute to cut out a notch in the stud that mirrored my stomach. When I finished, I stepped through the hole with confidence and easily slid between the stud and the wall, my stomach comfortably fitting the shape I'd cut out of the two-by-four. It was a simple matter of reaching over and turning the valves on again. As I slid back past the stud and stepped out through the hole in the wall, I felt an odd mixture of pride, relief, and thanksgiving. "Thank you, Father," I said. Alfred Hitchcock may have been my inspiration, but it was the Lord who reminded me about him.

All the while as I told George the story, he stood there by the hedge, smiling and chuckling at the situation I'd managed to get myself into. "Thanks for the advice, George," I said. "I've never turned off the outside faucets. There aren't any valves to do it."

But, just to play it safe, I swore off doughnuts.

TWO JOES

Jesus has a special place in his heart for children. When people brought children to Jesus that he might touch them, his disciples rebuked those who brought them.

> *But when Jesus saw it, he was much displeased, and said unto them, Suffer the little children to come unto me, and forbid them not: for of such is the kingdom of God. Verily I say unto you, Whosoever shall not receive the kingdom of God as a little child, he shall not enter therein. And he took them up in his arms, put his hands on them, and blessed them.*
>
> (Mark 10:14–16)

Christ was not saying that we cannot enter the kingdom of God unless we are childish. The Bible warns against childishness:

> *When I was a child, I spake as a child, I understood as a child, I thought as a child: But when I became a man, I put away childish things. For now we see through a glass, darkly; but then face to face: now I know in part; but then shall I know even as also I am known.*
> (1 Corinthians 13:11–12)

My friend Jeff McHugh always got a laugh out of me when he'd say, "You're only young once, but you can be immature forever." There is an innocence and wonder in small children that we all need when approaching God. I believe that Christ was telling us that we must be childlike, not childish.

The old hymns sing of Christ's love of children:

> *Jesus loves the little children*
> *All the children of the world*
> *Red and yellow, black and white, all are precious in his sight*
> *Jesus loves the little children of the world*[3]

And:

> *Jesus loves me this I know, for the Bible tells me so*
> *Little ones to him belong; they are weak and he is strong*
> *Yes, Jesus loves me, Yes, Jesus loves me*
> *Yes, Jesus loves me, the Bible tells me so*[4]

As adults, we tend to look at the current crop of children as inferior to children when we were little. Our memories are very selective.

> *You know you're getting old when you start to say*
> *I don't know what's the matter with these kids today.*[5]

We need to see children as Christ sees them, and be refreshed by their openness and honesty if we are to enter the kingdom of God.

We'd been dodging bullets all winter. Earlier in the season the major snowstorms tracked to our north, heading across upper New England and slamming into Boston before heading out to sea. Then the upper air currents shifted due to the El Nino effect, and the storms all passed to our south, hitting the mid-Atlantic states. Southern Connecticut was having a relatively snow-free winter. The storm that brought DC more than two feet of snow didn't produce a snow flurry around here. The forecast for yesterday predicted we would once again escape the heavy snowfall with the center of the storm passing to our north.

And then our luck ran out. What was supposed to be a light snow with an accumulation of no more than three to four inches dumped a foot of snow on our area. After almost twenty-four hours of snowfall, the snow finally stopped. I was getting ready to head out to tackle the driveway and sidewalk. By then it was dark out, and I was surprised to hear our doorbell ring. When I got to the door, I looked out the window on the top of the door, but couldn't see anyone. When I opened it, there were two little kids standing there looking like they were about to turn into twin pillars of ice. They looked eleven or twelve years old.

"Hey, Mister, do you want your driveway shoveled?" the smaller of the two boys asked.

"No thanks," I replied. "I have a snowblower and I was just about ready to go out to do it myself."

"Aw, c'mon," the other boy said. "We've been walking all over the neighborhood and we haven't been able to get a single job. All the big kids got there before us."

I knew what he was talking about. There are several teenagers in the neighborhood who go from door to door, asking to shovel driveways. When the doorbell rang, I figured it was a couple of them. I've always told them that I do it myself, so I think they've given up on ever getting any work from me.

As the boys stood there in the dark, the wind biting through their light sweat jackets, they were jumping up and down like little jack-in-the-boxes, trying to keep warm.

"Please, mister?" the smaller boy asked. "We've been out a long time and nobody will give us work."

"How much do you want, to do the sidewalk and driveway?" I asked.

"I don't know," the smaller boy said. "How much can you pay us?"

I stood there looking at the two shivering little kids and wondered if they could even handle such a heavy snow.

"I'll give you twenty dollars," I said.

"Okay," they chimed in unison. "That's good," and they waded through the snow on the lawn to get down to the driveway, shovels over their shoulders.

After about five minutes the doorbell rang again. I knew they couldn't have finished the sidewalk and driveway that quickly. This time it was the bigger kid—bigger, not taller.

"We can't do this big driveway and your sidewalk for twenty dollars," he said. "The snow's a foot deep." They'd done a single shovel-width path down the sidewalk and hadn't gotten very far on the driveway.

"This is really hard!" the smaller kid called up from the driveway.

I knew it was going to be a big job for them. They weren't much over four feet tall and there's a retaining wall along the sides of our driveway, so they'd have to throw the snow six feet in the air to get it up onto the lawn. With a foot of snow on the shovel, the math didn't work.

"I know the snow's heavy, but I have a guy who will plow my driveway for twenty-five dollars," I said. "It doesn't make any sense to pay you more than twenty dollars. I was on my way out to do the job with my snowblower when you came, so I could do it myself.

"I tell you what I'll do," I said. "You can leave that heavy mound of snow by the street that the snow plow pushed into the driveway. I'll give you the twenty dollars to shovel the rest of it."

I know how heavy the snow is that the plow pushes into my driveway, and it's a good six feet in from the street. The snow there was over two feet deep and I knew they couldn't handle it.

"Okay," they said, and I stepped back inside. Their spirit was willing but their flesh was short.

Fifteen minutes later, I put on my jacket and a cap, grabbed a pair of gloves, and headed down into the garage to get the snowblower. I could see the kids were really exhausted, but they were determined to finish the job. When I opened the garage door, there was a strip about six feet wide that they hadn't shoveled yet, right next to the garage door, so I grabbed my snow shovel and started working on it. The retaining wall is at its highest at that end of the driveway, and there was another two feet of snow already piled up on top of that. When I started shoveling, the littler kid came over and said, "We can shovel that, mister."

"Naw, that's all right! I'll get it. Just finish up what you've got left to do," I told him.

"No, you're paying us to do this, so I'll help you. Where can I put the snow?" he said.

"You have to throw it up over the wall."

"It'll just fall back down," he replied.

And sure enough, the first shovelful he tried to throw onto the top of the wall came cascading back down and he almost disappeared into a cloud of snow. He wasn't deterred, though. He just reached back for strength into his thin, shivering frame and took the next shovelful. This time he got it high enough to stay up.

"You know, I could have done this myself, but I remember what it was like when I was a kid and nobody would hire me to work," I said to the heavyset kid.

"Did you used to do this when you were a kid?" he asked.

"Sure did. I got paid a dollar or a dollar and a half."

"A dollar?" he asked incredulously. "I wouldn't shovel this driveway for a dollar!"

"You got to realize this was a long time ago. Candy bars cost a nickel and a double-scoop ice-cream cone was ten cents. Now a two-scoop ice cream cone costs more like two and a half bucks. I could go to a movie, buy a big soda, a large box of popcorn, and a candy bar and have change left over," I said.

He had to think about that, so he just kept shoveling. When I told them I wanted more than a path shoveled on each side of our two cars, the heavier kid turned his attention to that. The little kid called over to him and said, "Shovel the snow up to the tires, but don't hit the car!" Someone had to be the foreman.

"We weren't supposed to get this much snow," the heavier kid said. "The weatherman really screwed up this time!"

"It's tough forecasting the weather around here," I said. "I was a weatherman on the radio for seven years."

"You were on television?" he said, obviously impressed.

"No," I said, "on the radio. But I've been on television a lot of times."

"Are you famous?" he asked.

"Not really," I said.

He paused for a moment and then asked, "Were you ever wrong?"

"Hey, if you're a weatherman around here, you're wrong a lot," I said. And we both laughed.

By then, we were just finishing up the shoveling, other than the six-foot-wide strip out by the street. I called the kids over and gave each of them their ten dollars. They seemed happy about it.

"I want to get your names and phone numbers," I said. "I usually do this myself, but if I can't sometime, I can give you a call."

The little kid answered first. "My name is Joe O'Connor and I live on Pleasant View," and he gave me his phone number. The heavier-set kid was next. "My name is Joe Myers and I live on Sentinel Hill," and he gave me his number.

"Two Joes?" I said. "That'll make it easy to remember."

Pleasant View and Sentinel Hill aren't right around the corner. No wonder they looked half frozen when they first showed up at our door. They'd been out trying to get someone to hire them for a long time.

"You kids better get on home; you look like you're freezing to death," I said. "Go home and get some rest."

"I'm going home to have a nice cup of hot chocolate," little Joe said.

Big Joe was busy trying to put his ten dollars into a small side pocket halfway down the leg of his pants. I watched them as they walked down the street and under the streetlight. They were talking very animatedly. They'd had a good night. For once the big kids didn't get all the jobs.

An hour later I went out to attack the snow-plowed drift at the end of my driveway. I have an electric snowblower, and if it could talk it would have said, "Hey, mister, I can't do all of this; this snow's too heavy." Snowblowers have feelings too, so I worked on the heavy drifts a little at a time, stopping to clean out the snowblower and give it a rest every couple of minutes. It ended up taking me more than half an hour. The two Joes would have collapsed in a heap long before they could move all that snow.

Just as I was finishing up, I heard the sound of a snowblower. Sure enough, there was one of the teenage boys from the neighborhood coming down the street with a large gas-powered snowblower.

He looked over at me and could see that I was just finishing up, so he turned the corner and headed down a side street. By then I figured that little Joe was on his second cup of hot chocolate. Chalk one up for the two Joes.

Suffer the little children.

HAMBURGER HEAVEN

What a gift it is to be able to see, and yet we so often sleepwalk through our days, never noticing God's presence. Jesus spoke to his disciples, telling them how blessed they were to be able to not only see, but to see as he saw.

> And he turned him unto his disciples, and said privately, Blessed are the eyes which see the things that ye see: For I tell you, that many prophets and kings have desired to see those things which ye see, and have not seen them; and to hear those things which ye hear, and have not heard them.
>
> (Luke 10:23–24)

Every once in a while, God allows us to see into the hearts and minds of strangers who we might otherwise have passed by, never noticing them. This was one of those occasions.

It had been a long day. Other than stopping back at the house to change our clothes after church, we'd been on the move since five o'clock in the morning. The afternoon was filled with the greatest of unexpected blessings. Our grandson's wife had given birth to a beautiful baby girl. As soon as we received the news, we went up to the hospital to welcome a new soul into the family. There are very few joys that can equal holding a newborn baby in your arms. Imagine how Mary must have felt holding Jesus. New life is sacred and it was a joy to be a part of the celebration.

Driving home with our hearts filled with thanksgiving, I realized that we didn't have anything prepared for supper. Coming down the hill from the hospital, I remembered a restaurant on a side street at the intersection—a place where we'd never eaten. We'd lived in the area for eight years without even considering it, but we were bone tired and needed some place to get something to eat.

"How about trying the Duchess for dinner?" I asked my wife, Ruth.

We were always complaining there weren't any good restaurants in the area. You had your choice of Burger King, Mackey D, Kentucky Fried Chicken, or pizza. We were driving right by Kentucky Fried Chicken, but we'd just had chicken from there the night before. We get food there so often I'm surprised we don't crow when the sun comes up in the morning.

"That's all right with me," she answered.

I took a left at the light and pulled into the parking lot.

When we walked up to the door, I could see that the Duchess was a little worse for wear. Being lost on a side street with a Burger King, a Quiznos, and a KFC at the intersection wasn't the ideal location. For a late Sunday afternoon, the restaurant was busy and there was a short line at the counter. The last time we were in a Duchess restaurant many years ago, I remember there being a fairly wide variety of meal choices. Either my memory is poor, or over the years the chain had evolved into a burger-and-fries fast-food, take-out restaurant with a choice of only three or four dinners. After standing there for a few minutes, we each decided on a dinner and placed our order. Neither one of us anticipated that we were about to have a wonderful experience, and it would have very little to do with the food.

When we placed our order, the man behind the counter told us we could take a seat and someone would bring our meal to us. Even though the restaurant was busy, most of the customers were there for takeout, so we had our choice of almost any table or booth in the restaurant. We picked a booth near the front of the restaurant, away from the hustle around the counter and were just settling in when our waitress magically appeared with our soup and salad on a tray.

"I brought your soup and salad," she said cheerily, and placed the tray on our table.

I looked up to see a little sparkle-eyed woman just this side of elderly. She would have had to stand on her tiptoes to reach five feet high. She busily transferred our food onto our table, chattering away, smiling all the while. Then she stepped back and looked at Ruth with a big grin.

"She's very beautiful, isn't she?" she said, giving me a wink and a little cock of her hips.

"She certainly is," I answered her, matching grin for grin.

"I'll be back with the rest of your dinner, as soon as it's up," she said, and was gone as quickly as she came.

Watching her as she scooted around the room, I had to smile. She was full of energy and had a few kind words to say to everyone as she brought their food. We had just about finished our soup and salad when she appeared again with our main course on a tray. She was very efficient and cleared off our plates with a quick flick of her wrist. She had to move fast because she seemed to be the only waitress in the restaurant. I wondered where she got her energy because she looked to be too old to be working as a waitress. I know how hard that job is for a young woman, and she looked older than me.

After we'd eaten most of our dinner I walked back to the counter, and she was standing there in a rare moment of inaction. I asked her if we could have a couple of take-out containers, and she quickly produced two of them from behind the counter.

"Would you like a bag to carry them in?" she asked as she handed me a bag.

"Thanks, I'd appreciate it," I said.

When we'd collected our food and were ready to leave, I reached in my billfold to get a couple of dollars to leave as a tip. The smallest bill I had was a five-dollar bill. I hesitated for a moment and then smiled. That would work, just fine. I asked Ruth to wait for a minute and walked back to the counter. Our waitress was standing there, holding a little coin purse in her hands. I figured that someone had left her a tip because she was opening her purse to put something in it. When she saw me, she smiled and stepped out from behind the counter.

"I was looking for you. I just wanted to give you a tip," I said, and handed her the folded-up five-dollar bill.

She looked at it as I handed it to her and said, "Oh, I can't take this! You can just give me a dollar."

"I don't have a dollar, and besides—you were so nice to us, this is what I wanted to give you."

The more she tried to give the bill back to me, the more I pushed her hand away. Finally, I gently took her hand between my two hands and smiled, looking deep into her eyes. I hadn't had a chance to slow her down enough to really look at her, but she had the most beautiful pale-blue eyes I'd ever seen There was something strangely familiar and ancient about them, as if I'd seen them somewhere before. Standing there talking with her, holding her hand and looking into her glistening blue eyes, everything around me went out of focus. After standing there for a moment completely transfixed by the experience, she gently removed her hand from mine, and smiled warmly.

"I'll take it for my birthday," she said, carefully tucking the folded bill into her change purse. "I just turned ninety."

I placed my hands gently on her shoulders and said, "Ninety! That's wonderful! Happy birthday! God bless you."

There are times in life when you're moving within an ordinary, everyday dimension and suddenly you feel as if you've stepped up to a higher, more spiritual, plane. It is very difficult to describe what happened that day, or even to understand it. Hundreds of people flow through that restaurant every day, and if they notice the waitress at all, they might momentarily wonder why such an old woman is still working before they go back to their cheeseburger and fries, talking about what was on television the other night. It would be as if they had never seen her, and in truth, they never had.

Christ spoke the truth when he said, "For where two or three are gathered together in my name, there am I in the midst of them" (Matthew 18:20). When Christ drops by, he can make an ordinary day holy.

THE SHEPHERD'S WATCH

In the beginning, God created sheep. Well, maybe not in the very beginning, but by the time Abel was born there were sheep. And sheep need a shepherd.

> And Adam knew Eve his wife; and she conceived, and bare Cain, and said, I have gotten a man from the Lord. And she again bare his brother Abel. And Abel was a keeper of sheep, but Cain was a tiller of the ground.
>
> (Genesis 4:1–2)

Throughout the Bible shepherds play an important part in the story of God and his relationship to man. The prophet Isaiah wrote of God coming to earth like a shepherd:

> Behold, the Lord God will come with strong hand, and his arm shall rule for him: behold, his reward is with him, and his work before him. He shall feed his flock like a shepherd: he shall gather the lambs with his arm, and carry them in his bosom, and shall gently lead those that are with young.
>
> (Isaiah 40:10–11)

Most people know about the prophet Ezekiel. He's the one who saw the wheel in the middle of the wheel. God revealed the future to Ezekiel. He spoke of King David, who was another in a long line of shepherds, and at the same time, he foretold the coming of the Good Shepherd, Jesus.

> *And I will set up one shepherd over them, and he shall feed them, even my servant David; he shall feed them, and he shall be their shepherd.*
> (Ezekiel 34:23)

On that holiest of nights when Christ was born, the first people the angels proclaimed his birth to were shepherds out in the fields watching over their flocks.

> *And there were in the same country shepherds abiding in the field, keeping watch over their flock by night. And lo, the angel of the Lord came upon them, and the glory of the Lord shone round about them: and they were sore afraid. . . . And it came to pass, as the angels were gone away from them into heaven, the shepherds said one to another, Let us now go even unto Bethlehem, and see this thing which is come to pass, which the Lord hath made known to us.*
> (Luke 2:8–9, 15)

In David's most beloved psalm, he speaks of the Lord as his shepherd. How many times have we turned to this image as a source of comfort?

> *The Lord is my shepherd; I shall not want. He maketh me to lie down in green pastures: he leadeth me beside the still waters. He restoreth my soul: he leadeth me in the paths of righteousness for his name's sake. Yea, though I walk through the valley of the shadow of death, I will fear no evil: for thou art with me; thy rod and thy staff they comfort me.*
> (Psalm 23:1–4)

Christ himself expresses his love through the imagery of a shepherd.

> *For the Son of man is come to save that which was lost. How think ye? If a man have a hundred sheep, and one of them be gone astray, doth he not leave the ninety and nine, and goeth into the mountains, and seeketh that which is gone astray? And if so be that he find it, verily I say unto you, he rejoiceth more of that sheep, than of the ninety and nine which went not astray.*
> (Matthew 18:11–13)

The Shepherd's Watch

Nowadays, we don't see shepherds' staffs unless they are a stage prop. In the movies, staffs are as tall as the shepherds, but most shepherd staffs weren't that big. They were no higher than a man's waist. Although the curved top of the staff was formerly used to wrap around the neck of a sheep to pull them back into the flock, the primary purpose of the staff was to provide support and balance when walking across uneven terrain. Staffs still provide that support and balance today for people who've lost much of the strength in their legs and find a level hallway to be a challenging terrain. Now we call them canes.

The cane said, "Buy me!" Or more accurately, it enticed me over to the table and said, "Why don't you put in a nice, high bid on me?" The cane was lying there on one of the long tables that had been set up for the auction, surrounded by pieces of pottery, books, and other odds and ends. I certainly wasn't looking for a cane. Even though I'm seventy-five, the Lord has blessed me with strong legs. Why would an able-bodied man want a cane? What initially drew me to it was that I knew Judy Goddard—the person who had created it. Judy hand-decorates wooden canes with Christian Scriptures and writings. I'd never seen one of the canes, and I was attracted to it the minute I spotted it. When I picked it up, I noticed it was a puzzle cane, and there was a trick to reading the quotation. There were no secret levers or panels to twist. It was more a matter of how you read it.

Scripture is like that. Sometimes the meaning is not revealed with a casual glance. I was happy to see the quotation she used, because it is one of my favorites: "Lord, make me an instrument of your peace. Where there is hatred, let me sow love" (St. Francis of Assisi).

When I looked at the sheet where you could write down your bid, I was relieved to see that no one had placed a bid yet. It was early in the first day of the auction, so I wasn't in any rush to make a bid. Besides, I wasn't sure why I wanted to get the cane. I didn't know anyone I could give it to, and I didn't see any need for it myself in the foreseeable future. As the day wore on, my wife and I were preoccupied, enjoying the music. We were at our first

Getaway—a folk festival presented by the Greater Washington Folksong Society. That afternoon we dropped by the auction tables again, and I noticed that a friend had placed a small bid on the cane. As I turned it slowly in my hand, admiring the craftsmanship and the quotation, I had conflicting thoughts. My friend uses a cane, and it seemed thoughtless to outbid her when, at least for the time being, I had no use for it. Once again, I placed the cane gently on the table and walked away. It wasn't until that night when I was lying in bed that the Lord talked to me about the cane. I hadn't made the connection between a cane and a shepherd's staff.

Many years ago when my father was still alive, my son Gideon and I made a cane for him. I was working at the Stamford Museum and Nature Center, and I was fascinated with the many young saplings in the woods with vines entwined around them. As the sapling grew, the bark underneath the vine was strangled, leaving a smooth spiral when the vine was removed. I'd seen a walking stick made from a sapling several years ago and thought Gideon and I could make a cane for my father.

Walking through the woods, we searched the openings where new saplings were growing until we found one just the right size with a vine spiraling around it. We cut it down with the handsaw I'd brought along, and carefully pulled the vine that was tightly wound around it, revealing the smooth wood underneath. Once we'd cut the trunk to an appropriate length, we sanded and polished the top for a knob and put a rubber cap on the bottom. It made a very handsome cane, just the right height for my father. On our next trip home, Gideon gave it to his grandpa, and my dad treasured that cane.

As it turned out, we'd made a rod, not a staff. It needed something on the top to hold on to, so my father cut a piece of wood for a handle and attached it to the top of the rod, making a serviceable cane. It took three generations of Rasmussen men to make it. He used it for years until he finally had to use a walker. The cane always got a lot of attention, and my father was very proud to tell the story about how his son and grandson made it for him. I thought of that cane that night, while lying there in bed conversing with the Lord.

My first thought when I picked up the cane earlier that day had been sobering. I treasure being able to walk, and being dependent on a cane was not something I was looking forward to. I felt the heft of the cane and tested it for its height. It was just the right size and felt strangely comfortable, but at the same time I resisted the idea that someday I might be dependent upon it. Standing there lost in thought, I remembered the chorus to a song I'd written—"Sweet, Quiet Peace"—that I was planning to sing in the gospel songs workshop the following morning. It gave me comfort.

> *One thing I know, and this for certain*
> *All will be well, no matter what the future holds*
> *He will be there to share my every burden*
> *And there's a sweet, quiet peace in my soul*

Instead of looking at the cane with trepidation, thinking about the day when I would no longer walk without one, I took comfort in knowing that whatever the future holds for me, I'll be all right, because Christ will be walking beside me.

> *Storms may rage, and dark clouds gather*
> *Sometimes my way is hard to see*
> *But in my heart, there's a calm assurance*
> *Because I know that he walks with me*

When we see images of Christ carrying a staff, it stands as tall as him. I can understand why he is depicted with such a tall staff. It would be disturbing to see a drawing of him walking with a waist-high cane because we associate canes with an injury or old age. In the years of his ministry, Christ walked everywhere he went, except for his triumphant entrance into Jerusalem on a donkey. He certainly didn't need a cane.

The next morning at the gospel songs workshop, I had a chance to talk with Judy Goddard and she told me how she'd come to make the canes. An elderly friend of hers was going on a cruise and asked her to decorate her cane with Christian symbols and Scripture as a blessing and protection. When she saw how pleased her friend was with her cane, she realized that she could bring the Lord's message to others in the same way and began crafting walking canes.

My friend who'd placed a bid on the cane was also at the gospel songs workshop, and I had a chance to talk with her. I told her that the Lord had put it on my heart to get the cane, but I was uncomfortable bidding against her. She assured me that it was all right if I outbid her. She didn't even know if she could fit the cane in her suitcase for her flight back to California. She already had three canes and didn't need a fourth one. When one o'clock in the afternoon rolled around, I was the high bidder and quickly paid for the cane before someone else showed up at the last minute to outbid me.

Looking at the cane leaning against my desk, I think of Jesus and I have to smile. I feel secure knowing that I am under the watchful eye of the Good Shepherd.

> I am the good shepherd: the good shepherd giveth his life for the sheep . . . . I am the good shepherd, and know my sheep, and am known of mine. As the Father knoweth me, even so know I the Father: and I lay down my life for the sheep. And other sheep I have, which are not of this fold: them also I must bring, and they shall hear my voice; and there shall be one fold, and one shepherd.
> (John 10:11, 14–16)

> If the day ever comes when I need a walking cane, it will be an old, familiar friend.

Over two thousand years ago, God answered our prayers and sent us his Good Shepherd. I know that no matter what the future holds, all will be well. Nothing can harm me. I am on the Good Shepherd's watch.

No harm will befall you on the Shepherd's watch[6]

A ROSE REMEMBERED

Nobody wants to be forgotten. When people talk about us after we're gone, we surely don't want them to say, "I'll never forget What's-his-name." But even the most famous names are soon forgotten. How many people recognize the name Billy Murray? He had 169 top forty hits from 1903 through 1927, and yet very few people remember him (Elvis had 113). His hits included "Meet Me in St. Louis, Louis," "Give My Regards to Broadway," "By the Light of the Silvery Moon," and "Alexander's Ragtime Band." Today, he's even less well known than What's-his-name. At best, fame is fleeting. But if you want to be remembered by anyone, it should be Jesus.

One of the most quoted Scriptures comes from Christ's crucifixion. Two thieves hung beside Christ on Golgotha. One of the thieves taunted Jesus, but the other came to his defense.

> But the other answering rebuked him, saying, Dost not thou fear God, seeing thou art in the same condemnation? And we indeed justly; for we receive the due reward for our deeds: but this man hath done nothing amiss.
>
> (Luke 23:40–41)

The thief did not ask for forgiveness, or to be saved from death. He asked Jesus to remember him.

And he said unto Jesus, Lord, remember me when thou comest into thy kingdom. And Jesus said unto him, Verily I say unto Thee, Today shalt thou be with me in paradise.

(Luke 23:42–43)

Nursing homes are filled with people who feel forgotten. They've outlived their friends and family and hunger for the most modest attentions. Like the thief on the cross, they ask to be remembered. Jesus remembers them, and comes to be with them at their bedside.

> *Jesus loves me, loves me still*
> *Thou I'm very weak and ill*
> *From his shining throne on high*
> *Comes to watch me where I lie[7]*

Jesus calls us to remember those who are confined in nursing homes. Our reward will be great.

> *Then shall the King say unto them on his right hand, Come, ye blessed of my Father, inherit the kingdom prepared for you from the foundation of the world . . . . I was sick, and ye visited me.*
>
> (Matthew 25:34, 36)

God will reward us when we stand before him, but our most immediate rewards come from those we visit. It is the sick who may appear to have so little left to give who bless us with their love and gratitude.

Rose Parks was a little woman. I'm not sure just how little she was because I never saw her out of her bed. Rosa Parks (no relation) was a little woman too, from what I remember. She changed history by sitting down.

I met Rose Parks in a nursing home. She was the roommate of Margaret's mother, a friend of ours. My wife and I visited her every Sunday after church. Margaret's mother had the walls on her side of the room covered with "get well" cards, "missing you" cards, photos, and handmade drawings from the kids in her family. The walls on Rose's side of the room were barren. Her husband had died years before and they had no children. Like many others in the nursing homes my wife and I visit, Rose had outlived her friends and was facing her final days alone. She was blessed to have Margaret's mother as a roommate because she was a positive, generous-spirited woman. When we'd stop by to visit, we always tried to spend a little time talking with Rose. We never once saw someone else visiting her.

One Sunday morning at church, Margaret told us that her mother had passed away. The image of Rose lying there alone in her room with no visitors to brighten her days really haunted me. The last few times we had visited the nursing home, Rose seemed especially upset when we were leaving. I think she was concerned that if Margaret's mother passed first, we'd stop coming to visit her. When we came over to her bed to give her a kiss and an embrace, she'd look pleadingly into our eyes, reach out her hand to touch us gently, and say, "Please don't forget me." It was heart-wrenching to hear the desperation in her voice.

The next few months we made our weekly visit to see Rose. She had become dear to us, and we were always lifted when we saw the excitement in her face when we walked through the door. We'd bring her small gifts to brighten her room, and somehow it didn't seem so barren anymore. In return, Rose gave us her love and gratitude. She always gave more than she received, lying flat on her back in the bed.

The day we dropped by to visit Rose and found her empty bed, we were very concerned. We held out hope that perhaps she had just been taken to another room for therapy or treatment, but our hearts were heavy. We found one of the nurses and asked, "Where is Rose?"

"No one told you?" she said. "Rose passed away yesterday."

"Do you know if there is going to be a funeral or memorial service for her?" we asked.

"I don't have any information, but if you check at the front desk, maybe they can tell you."

A couple of days later we called the nursing home and were told there was going to be a memorial service at the funeral home where her body was being prepared for interment. When we arrived at the funeral home the next day, we were ushered into a small room where the memorial service was to be held. Looking around the room at the small scattering of people sitting in folding chairs, I thought of Rose's plea: "Please don't forget me!"

The memorial service was short, and after the service we talked briefly with a couple of the other people who'd come. There were three or four people from the church she had attended when she was in better health, and a neighbor or two, and us, and Margaret.

Ten years have passed and we haven't forgotten Rose. Her gentle spirit and appreciation for small attentions were a great joy to us. "But the fruit of the Spirit is love, joy, peace, long-suffering, gentleness, goodness, faith" (Galatians 5:22). All these things Rose gave to us. Good people are never forgotten.

T-SHIRT TESTIMONY

In Roman times, if you spoke the word Jesus in mixed company, you might have ended up being thrown to the lions. Despite the danger, countless early Christians went to their death praising Jesus's name. They spoke out, expressing their love for Christ, no matter what the consequences. These days, with all the concern about being politically correct and not offending nonbelievers we are too often driven by concern for what man will think of us, not God.

Christ spoke clearly about the importance of testifying for him:

> *Also I say unto you, whosoever shall confess me before men, him shall the Son of man also confess before the angels of God.*
> (Luke 12:8)

The Five Blind Boys of Mississippi sang with great conviction, "If I cannot speak for Jesus, I'd rather die."[8] *Silence was not an option for them. They found their voice in song. Others speak for Jesus more quietly. Jesus calls all those who believe in him to testify, each in his own way.*

> *If I cannot sing like angels*
> *If I cannot preach like Paul*
> *I can tell the love of Jesus*
> *And how he died for all*[9]

Some are called to preach from a magnificent pulpit in a soaring cathedral, some on a barstool. Some are too quiet-natured to speak out in public. Some just wear a T-shirt.

Today someone finally commented on my T-shirt. I got the T-shirt when the men's chorus at Union Baptist Church performed their annual concert three years ago. Every year as part of the weekend Men's Day Celebration there is a picnic, and all the men wear matching T-shirts. I particularly liked this one. It says "Jesus: That's my final answer." The word *Jesus* is in red block letters almost six inches tall, so you can't miss it. I've worn the T-shirt many times, but no one has ever commented about it until today. When I walked into my exercise class this morning, Kathy, our instructor, came over to me and said, "I've got to look at your T-shirt."

"You're the first one who has ever said anything about it," I said.

"Maybe they're afraid that you're an evangelist," she responded.

I had to laugh at that.

"The only thing I'd change is I'd say 'He is the only answer,' " she said, and I agreed.

Summer is T-shirt weather for me, and my Jesus shirt is in regular rotation with several others. Most of them generate a comment every now and then. None can match my Boston Red Sox shirt, though.

Last summer, there was a crew working down the corner from our house. They were tearing up the street a few lots at a time, laying in a new water line. As irritations go, this one was not much to get wound up about. Every once in a while I'd have to drive around the block to go somewhere because the street would be blocked off, and occasionally they'd shut off the water, but other than that it was no real bother. When I saw that they were nearing the end of the street, I walked over to a couple of the guys working in the trench.

"How you coming along down there?" I asked.

"We're doing fine. We should finish up tomorrow," one of the men answered. And then he noticed that I was wearing my Red Sox T-shirt.

"You a Red Sox fan?" he asked.

"Yeah, why?" I answered, in a friendly tone of voice. I was used to people giving me a hard time whenever I wore my Red Sox T-shirt. Our town is less than a hundred miles from New York City, so Yankees fans outnumber Red Sox fans about fifty to one.

"You see that truck over there? The guy sitting in the truck is a big Red Sox fan. Go over and show him your T-shirt. He'll really like it."

I walked over to the truck, and when I came around to the other side, I saw this big, burly guy almost spilling out of the cab, one arm heavily draped over the open window. "The Yankees suck!" I yelled, with a big grin on my face. And then I realized I'd been set up. The guy was a big Yankees fan. At first he scowled menacingly at me, and then we both burst out laughing. By then, the two guys had climbed out of the ditch and appeared around the back of the truck, doubled over with laughter.

"Thanks a lot, guys! I coulda had my head knocked off!"

"We just wanted to see if we could get him out of that truck. He's been sitting in there all day!" And we all laughed.

"You don't like my Red Sox T-shirt?" I asked. "Hey, tomorrow I'll wear my Yankees T-shirt if that'll make you happy. Or if you'd like, I can wear my Cleveland Indians T-shirt with my Chicago Cubs cap, or my Pittsburgh Pirates shirt and cap. I can even wear my Yankees T-shirt with my Red Sox cap." By then, we were all having a big laugh. That was reason enough to make me happy that I'd worn the T-shirt. Lifelong friendships have started on flimsier grounds. That's how I'd met Dwayne.

I had just started graduate school at Columbia University and didn't know a soul. A few days after classes began I was on my way up to my room in the dorm when the elevator stopped and a guy stepped in carrying a Gene Autry guitar. I don't remember what I said, but it was probably something dumb like, "You play guitar?" I'd like to think it was something cleverer like, "So, where's your Hopalong Cassidy lunch box?" Whatever I said, it started a conversation. When we finally got around to introducing ourselves, it turned out Dwayne was another Midwesterner—he was from Kansas. As we talked, we discovered we had more in common than playing guitar and singing folk music. Both of us had Korean roommates. After a few minutes of conversation, we decided to see if we could get my roommate to move in with Dwayne's so that Dwayne and I could share a room. Even though it was against the rules, I convinced the office to let us make the switch, and in the process a lifetime friendship was formed. I was Dwayne's best man when he married a few years later. It had all started with Gene Autry.

The thing is, I don't wear a T-shirt with a logo or saying on it to get a rise out of anyone. I wear it because I like how the shirt looks or because of what it says. In the case of my Jesus shirt, I wear it because when I have something good in my life, I want to share it. Normally, I don't even like to talk about my faith unless the Lord opens the door. I certainly don't wear the shirt with any expectation of converting someone, any more than my friend Dwayne was carrying his Gene Autry guitar trying to convert me to believing in Gene. I was always a Roy Rogers fan, myself. I'd take Gabby Hayes over Smiley Burnett any day.

What strikes me is that people are so passionate about their baseball team, and yet never say a word when I wear my Jesus shirt. It can't be that they're offended because they're rooting for the other side. The only Devil T-shirt I've seen is one for the New Jersey Devils. Why is it that people don't say anything? I can understand people who aren't Christian not saying something, but what about all the Christians? It would be nice if every once in a while someone said, "Hey, I like your T-shirt! I love Jesus too." It would open a conversation, and a stranger might become a friend. You never know what God is going to use to bring lovers of the Lord together.

That brings me back to Kathy. As I found out, she is a Christian writer and has published a book. I never would have known that if I hadn't worn that T-shirt.

What I really need is a T-shirt that says "Jesus Loves the Red Sox," with a smaller line underneath it that says, "and the Yankees too."

JESUS LOVES RED SOX ICE CREAM?

*Y*ou never know where the opportunity for a ministry is going to arise. Not all sermons are delivered from a pulpit.

After I finished the rough draft for the chapter "T-Shirt Testimony," I posted it on Facebook to share with my friends. Michelle Jones, who is a member of the church my wife and I belong to, spotted a line that caught her attention: "What I really need is a T-shirt that says 'Jesus Loves the Red Sox,' with a smaller line underneath it that says, 'And the Yankees, Too.'"

Michelle has a company that produces T-shirts and other items with Christian messages, in addition to items for businesses, churches, and other organizations. She loved the idea for the Red Sox T-shirt and offered to make one for me. I was delighted with the offer and ordered one for my friend Rev. Ken Smith. He is a great Red Sox fan, but he knows the truth of the message, "Jesus loves." What I didn't know at the time was how many sidewalk conversations I would have about those two powerful words. Like most people, I can't imagine myself standing up on a soapbox (if they even make them anymore) on a street corner saying, "Jesus loves" to everyone who passes by. As it turns out, all I have to do is wear my T-shirt and evangelism comes to me.

This whole Yankees/Red Sox rivalry is getting downright ridiculous. I was standing in the checkout line at the supermarket the other day when I noticed the woman behind me had two quarts of Red Sox ice cream. I turned to her and asked, "You're not buying Yankees ice cream?"

"Hell no!" she said loudly. "I can't stand the Yankees! There's no way I'd ever eat that stuff!"

She should have been more concerned about what was coming out of her mouth than what she was putting in it.

> Not that which goeth into the mouth defileth a man; but that which cometh out of the mouth, this defileth a man.
> (Matthew 15:11)

"I'm sorry I'm not wearing my Jesus loves the Red Sox T-shirt," I said. A smile spread across her face. Suddenly, I was a kindred spirit. And then I added, "The full message is, 'Jesus loves the Red Sox, and the Yankees, too.'"

"Hmppff!" she muttered, with a look of disgust on her face as she slammed her two gallons of Red Sox ice cream onto the conveyor belt. I could see she was in no mood to talk to a Yankees fan. She'd missed the whole point. I've never been a Yankees fan, but Jesus loves everyone, and that includes Yankees fans. If they're good enough for Jesus, they're good enough for me. Who would ever imagine anyone would get so emotional about a gallon of ice cream named after a rival team? I could tell this conversation would go nowhere, so I paid my bill and smiled at her as I turned to leave. I didn't want to get hit upside the head with a flying gallon of Red Sox ice cream.

The next time I was in the supermarket, I went over to the ice cream freezer to look at the Yankees and Red Sox ice creams. There they were, sitting in perfect peace right next to each other on the shelf. You'd never think such innocent-looking containers could generate such hateful emotions. Out of curiosity, I pulled out a gallon of Yankees ice cream to see what flavor it was. Printed on the side of the container was a proud pronouncement that the ice cream had "Traditional Yankees Pinstripes." The flavor of the ice cream was "Pinstripe Brownie Blast!" I've never seen brown Yankee pinstripes. There were just a couple of gallons of Yankees ice cream on the shelf, and just that one flavor. The freezer shelves were loaded with Red Sox ice cream in three different flavors: "Grand Slam Vanilla," "BoSox Brownie," and "Comeback Caramel." Red Sox fans living in Yankees country have a much wider choice of flavors. On the bottom shelf, all frosted with freezer burn, was a lonely gallon of Phillies "Graham Slam" ice cream. How it ever ended up in a freezer in an IGA supermarket in Connecticut is beyond me.

Yankee fans may find this whole discussion problematical, but they can order "Jesus loves the Yankees, and the Red Sox, too" T-shirts from Michele Jones by contacting her at Michelle@SenojCustomProducts.com. Michelle and her family are all Yankee fans and they proudly wear their "Jesus loves the Yankees, and the Red Sox, too" T-shirts. I have no idea what kind of ice cream they eat. The safest policy is: don't ask, don't tell.

WHERE TWO OR THREE ARE GATHERED

*W*e are all impressed by numbers. TV evangelists preach to tens of thousands of people in their congregations, and hundreds of thousands more watch their services on television. In comparison, Christ's ministry was far more modest. From Jerusalem in the south to Christ's northernmost journeys to Tyre and Caesarea, his ministry covered a distance of only about one hundred miles. While Christ spoke at times to crowds of as many as five thousand and performed two of his most memorable miracles feeding the multitudes with a few loaves of bread and two or three fish, he more commonly spoke to small crowds as he traveled through the country. Jesus was very much a local prophet. His ministry was done on foot, and his followers were everyday folk he met along the way. As the word of his miracles spread, the sick and the lame would call out to him as he was passing by, asking for a healing.

> And they came to Jericho; and as he went out of Jericho with his disciples and a great number of people, blind Bartimaeus, the son of Timeus, sat by the highway side begging. And when he heard that it was Jesus of Nazareth, he began to cry out, and say, Jesus, thou son of David, have mercy on me. And many charged that he should hold his peace; but he cried the more a great deal, Thou son of David, have mercy on me. And Jesus stood still, and commanded him to be called.

And they called the blind man, saying unto him, Be of good comfort; rise; he calleth thee. And he, casting away his garment, rose, and came to Jesus. And Jesus answered and said unto him, What would thou that I should do unto thee? The blind man said unto him, Lord, that I might receive my sight. And Jesus said unto him, Go thy way, thy faith hath made thee whole, And immediately he received his sight, and followed Jesus in the way.

(Mark 10:46–52)

Somewhere along the way in the old gospel song, Blind Bartimaeus became Blind Barnabus. Barnabus was actually a companion of Paul, so his name would have been familiar to those who read the Bible.

> *Old blind Barnabus stood on the way*
> *Old blind Barnabus stood on the way*
> *Old blind Barnabus stood on the way*
> *Crying Oh, Lordy, have mercy on me*[10]

If Christ were preaching today, you'd be as likely to hear him in a supermarket parking lot as you would in a large cathedral. He still shows up where you least expect to find him, and he makes his presence known in the hearts of those who love him.

It was five minutes before seven, and other than my wife and the director of the library, no one had arrived to the "Meet the Author" evening I was hosting for my book *The Gate of Beautiful*. The table in the back of the room was graciously spread with cheese and crackers and a variety of cookies, and the coffee pot gurgled invitingly, the aroma filling the room. Just when it looked as if no one was going to come, two women came hurriedly down the stairs and entered the room. I could see them as they came in because the large double doors in the back of the room were open. One woman was walking with a cane, and it was clear she'd been rushing. As they entered the room, I smiled broadly and called out to them, "Welcome! Come on in! I was wondering if anyone was coming. 'Where two or three are gathered . . .' "[11] I didn't need to finish the sentence. We all knew who would be there.

"There was an accident on Route 8," one of the women offered. "We got stuck in traffic for a half an hour."

That didn't bode well for the attendance. It was already raining, and when we arrived, the parking lot was almost empty.

By then it was just after seven, and I asked Elspeth, the library director, if she minded if we had a cup of coffee and a cookie or two before I started. Maybe we'd pick up a few more people. No sooner than I'd poured myself a cup of coffee than another woman came hurriedly down the stairs. I asked her, "Did you get tied up on Route 8?"

And she said, "No, I just had to drive down the hill to get here."

By the time I was ready to start, Joyce arrived. We'd met Joyce at church a couple of weeks ago and asked her to come and sit with us, as she was new to the church. We were glad to see her.

I started the program talking about how I'd come to write my book, and my love of stories. The first song I sang was "Just Because You Like to Do It, That Don't Make It Right." The song has an old country-blues shuffle to it and tells the stories of Noah and Jonah. I wanted to warm up the people. It was a chilly, blustery night, and I appreciated people coming out in such unwelcoming weather. I followed the song by reading a passage of Scripture about a man who'd been crippled for thirty-eight years, who still hadn't given up hope of being cured. One day Christ passed by the pools of Bethesda where the man was lying on a pallet.

> When Jesus saw him lie, and knew that he had been now a long time in that case, he said unto him, Wilt thou be made whole? . . . Jesus saith unto him, rise, take up thy bed and walk.
> (John 5:6, 8)

I've always been moved by that story, and I talked about it awhile before I sang the song I wrote titled "Healing Waters." The story is one of the great testimonies of faith. It is hard not to get discouraged when we are suffering and it seems that God is indifferent to our prayers. When I played the song, I noticed Joyce was wiping tears from her eyes. I was very moved to see her reaction to the song. It's one I've seen before when I've performed the song at nursing homes.

Lay me down in the healing waters
Cleanse my soul of every sin
Lift me up, that I might walk with Thee
Oh Lord, make me whole again

"We all need to be laid in the healing waters of Christ's love," I said. "Some of us need a physical healing, and all of us need a spiritual healing." At that moment, I felt a love flowing through the room, drawing us together.

As I continued to talk and read passages from my book, we were interrupted by a man scrambling down the stairs. He looked wet and a little bedraggled, but he had a warm smile on his face, and I called out to him, "C'mon in! I'm glad you could make it!" The man looked like he was in his early or mid fifties. When he smiled, his enthusiasm spread through the room.

As the evening wore on, the words to the songs seemed to be a comfort to all who were gathered there. When I sang about Jesus, the carpenter's son, the verse about healing offered words of great hope.

He will show mercy to the forsaken
He will bring comfort to those who mourn
To the afflicted, He will bring healing
And to the weary, He will bring rest[12]

I felt wrapped in the warmth of those words.

I finished with "Sweet, Quiet Peace." I wrote the song remembering Christ's promise: "Peace I leave with you, my peace I give unto you; not as the world giveth, give I unto you" (John 14:27).

The chorus of the song expresses confidence in that promise:

One thing I know, and this for certain
All will be well, no matter what the future holds
He will be there to share your every burden
You'll find a sweet, quiet peace in your soul

After the program, everyone wanted to talk. I walked back to speak to the young man who had arrived so late. He greeted me with a warm smile and shook my hand. He spoke very enthusiastically about my guitar playing.

"I was watching your hand and how you finger-picked the strings," he said, and he motioned with his right hand. "I see that sometimes you also brush the strings like this," demonstrating with his hand. "I used to play guitar a little, but I've broken my arm twice, and now I can't close my hand with enough strength to form the chords." He held up his left hand and tried to curl his fingers around an imaginary guitar neck.

"Are you on computer?" I asked. "If you go to my website, you can hear a lot of my music that's posted there."

"I'm homeless," he said, as if it was of no great significance. "I walked up the hill tonight to come to the library, and I could hear the music when I came in, so I ran down the stairs to catch it. I'll go on the computer here in the library here and check it out," he added.

As I worked my way to the table in the back of the room to get a second cup of coffee and a plate of cheese and crackers, the woman who had arrived shortly after the first two women came over to talk with me.

"Are you going to have some cookies?" she asked in a friendly voice.

"No thanks, I can't; I'm diabetic," I told her.

"My mother was diabetic, and she had to watch what she ate," she responded. "She finally died from it."

"I'm so sorry to hear that," I said. "Did this happen recently?"

"In August," she answered, and I could see her fighting the tears.

"That's recent," I said.

After that, my wife and I talked awhile with Joyce. We were happy to see her. She'd been looking for a church home and we were happy that she'd come to First Baptist where we often go. She especially liked the song "Healing Waters." A couple of days after the program at the library, I received a call from Jan at church giving us the names of those who'd asked to be put on the prayer chain.

The first one was Joyce. She's been having serious problems with the nerves in her back. Sometimes when she walks, her nerves go numb, and when that happens, she falls down without warning. No wonder she responded so strongly to the song "Healing Waters."

It was a small turnout. Five loaves of bread and a couple of fishes would have fed our little gathering. There was no need for a miracle. The cookies and cheese and crackers were more than enough. But there was a greater feeding that occurred that night. I believe everyone went home filled with the Holy Spirit. And despite the serious concerns that were brought to that little room, there was a confidence knowing that Christ was there. Somehow, the future seemed less threatening,

> *One thing I know, and this for certain*
> *All will be well, no matter what the future holds*
> *He will be there to share our every burden*
> *Sweet, quiet peace*

And there was a sweet, quiet peace in our souls.

THE MEASURE OF MAN

Dreams have a bad rap. When you share your plans for the future with someone else, you're likely to be greeted with "Yeah, in your dreams!" or "Dream on!" The Loving Spoonful sang "What a Day for a Daydream" and the whole song was about lying in the sun and being a "lazy bulldog." Cute boys used to be called "dreamy" or "dreamboats." Fats Domino knew about dreamboats. He sang about one in "When My Dreamboat Comes Home." The dictionary holds a rather skeptical view of dreamers. Look at these definitions:[13]

> *"One who lives in a world of fancy or imagination."*
> *"One who has ideas or conceives projects regarded as impractical."*

But it wasn't always that way.

God's most common way of appearing to the prophets was in a dream. Having a vision was an honored way to receive revelations from God. The Bible ends with a whole book of revelations.

There was a time when great men were defined by their dreams. When you hear the words "I have a dream," you immediately think of Dr. Martin Luther King, Jr. There were those who thought his dream of racial equality was impractical or unrealistic. And just in case it wasn't, they were going to do everything in their power to make sure it was.

The prophet Joel spoke about the last days and the pouring out of God's spirit:

And it shall come to pass afterward, that I will pour out my spirit upon all flesh; and your sons and your daughters shall prophesy, your old men shall dream dreams, your young men shall see visions.

(Joel 2:28)

As long as there are dreamers, men will rise to greatness.

My wife and I were passing time in the Amsterdam airport, waiting for our flight to the United States. We'd disembarked from our cruise ship earlier that day after a twelve-day cruise of Scandinavia and northern Europe, and even though we'd had a wonderful time, we were anxious to get home. Our flight wasn't due to leave for two hours, so we wandered through the terminal looking for a place to eat. We stopped at a small café, and when our order was ready I set off, tray in hand, looking for a place where we could sit down. After I made two circles through the eating area, I found there wasn't an empty table in sight. When I noticed a woman sitting alone at a table for four, I motioned Ruth to follow me and walked over to the table.

"Excuse me. There don't seem to be any empty tables. Do you mind if we join you?" I asked.

"Not at all," she replied. "I was about to get up."

"There's no need for you to get up," I said. "Why don't you stay here and sit awhile with us?"

She gave us a warm smile, moved her tray to the side, and settled back down.

At first our conversation involved the usual pleasantries—exchanging names and where we were going. Marilyn had been on our cruise, although with two thousand passengers on board we hadn't met her. She was flying to St. Paul/Minneapolis, and we were flying to Detroit. I told her I had family in Minneapolis, and Ruth and I had been up to visit Mall America. When I told her that I'd grown up in Wisconsin, Marilyn told me that she had too.

"Where in Wisconsin?" I asked

"It's a little town," she said." You've probably never heard of it: Milton."

"Milton!" I exclaimed excitedly. "My mother grew up there! I spent many long summer days in Milton when I was a kid."

I told her that several years ago my wife and I went on a tour of the Milton House and were ushered into an orientation room to watch a video about the history of the building. When the opening title flashed on the screen, a song began playing, telling how Milton was first founded. My wife looked at me and said, "That sounds like you!" And it was. I had written a song, "Paradise Found," many years ago and sent a tape to the Milton Historical Society. I never heard back from them and figured the tape had long since disappeared.

When the docent came into the room to take us on our tour, I said, "That's me singing 'Paradise Lost' at the beginning of your video."

"It is?" she replied. "We just found a tape in a drawer and had no idea where it came from. Wait until I tell the director!" When we walked back into the gift shop area, I was introduced to the staff as if I were visiting royalty.

Marilyn seemed to be getting a kick out of the story as I was telling it. "Oh, I'll have to tell my brother and a friend of mine who still lives in Milton that I met you!" And suddenly we were lost in conversation about Milton.

My wife excused herself at that point and went to do some shopping in one of the small shops in the terminal, and Marilyn and I continued on with our conversation. I was surprised to discover that Marilyn knew so much of the history of Milton. Who would think such a small Midwestern farm town would have such an interesting past?

When I was growing up, Milton was less than one thousand in population. It only had two stop signs, so you could drive through without even noticing the town. I don't remember hearing a lot about Milton's history when I was a kid, even though I spent a lot of time there and went to Milton College for one year. If someone mentioned Joe Goodrich's name, the man who founded Milton,

I don't remember it. The thing that ultimately made me want to learn more was an experience I had one summer when I was home visiting my family. I was driving through Milton and just getting up to speed after the first stop sign when I looked across the park in the center of the town and was shocked to see a bar. The bar itself wasn't particularly striking; it was the fact that there was a bar in Milton. Let me tell you the story.

Like Martin Luther King Jr., Joseph Goodrich had a dream. Goodrich fought in the War of 1812 and rose to the rank of major. After the war he opened a small grocery store in Alfred, New York. But the major's dreams were too big for Alfred. He dreamt of founding a community of hardworking, teetotaling, upstanding Christians, and once he had saved enough money from the profits from his store, he was ready to leave. In July of 1838, Goodrich and two friends packed up their wagons and headed west.

> *Ships on the prairies that never sailed the seas*
> *Carrying all that they owned*
> *Sailing for mountains that they'll never reach*
> *Sailing away to home*[14]

When they reached southern Wisconsin, they marveled at the beauty of the country and the rich, fertile prairie soil. They knew they had found their home. Goodrich staked his claim on the eastern edge of what is now Milton, and one of his friends claimed land just to the west. There was never a question what Goodrich wanted to name his new town. He was a great admirer of John Milton and his book *Paradise Lost*, and in his honor, Goodrich named the town Paradise Found. He and his friends certainly hadn't traveled a thousand miles looking for Paradise Lost.

One of the first things Goodrich did was donate twenty acres of land for a park in the center of town. To encourage settlers traveling through the area to set their roots in Milton, he offered plots of land on the edge of the park to any man who was willing to take the "Cold Water Pledge."

*He bought twenty acres of prime prairie land for a
park in the center of town
He paid sixty dollars in trade from his store and
he named it Paradise Found
He gave parcels of land at the edge of the park to
any industrious man
Who was willing to swear to the Cold Water
pledge to drive King Alcohol from the land*[15]

Goodrich was a teetotaler and a member of the Cold Water Society. The pledge came from the Cherokee Nation that first formed the Cherokee Cold Water Army to combat alcoholism. The pledge that Major Goodrich required all the new merchants of the town to take was this:

> We hereby solemnly pledge ourselves that we will never use, nor buy, nor sell, nor give, nor receive as a drink, any whisky, brandy, rum, gin, wine, fermented cider, strong beer, or any kind of intoxicating liquors.

That was quite a mouthful.

Goodrich, being a good businessman, realized that the strategic location of the town at the crossroads of two trade routes offered many opportunities for the town to grow. A great innovator, Goodrich built a hexagonal free-standing grout hotel: the Milton House. It was one of the first free-standing concrete buildings in the country. To quench the thirst of weary, dust-covered travelers, the hotel had a temperance saloon where no liquor was served. The joke was that if someone wanted a stiff drink, they could go out to the well behind the hotel and pull up a bucket of cold Milton "rum."

*In just seven years, the town was alive,
 with shops up and down the street
There were blacksmiths and wheelwrights,
dry goods and drug stores, a post office, a plow factory
And over at Goodrich's temperance saloon,
the music and laughter would flow*

> *And they'd raise up their glasses of cold Milton rum,*
> *and offer the major a toast*[16]

If Goodrich's dream of a Utopian society was to succeed, the town would need an academy of learning, so Goodrich started the Milton Academy, which became Milton College. A staunch Seventh-Day Baptist, he also built the first church in Milton. Goodrich was more than an idle dreamer. He was committed to making those dreams come true. He was also a committed abolitionist and an active participant in the Underground Railway. The small log cabin that still stands behind the Milton House was a hideaway for runaway slaves. An underground tunnel connected the cabin to the basement of the hotel and provided a sleeping area for the runaways.

All was well for many years and the small town thrived, but as new people moved in there were some who had a thirst that cold water couldn't cure. In 1857, Isaac Morgan founded Milton Junction, a suburb of a town of only a few hundred people at that time. Morgan's vision was not Goodrich's, and a saloon was built in Milton Junction.

> *So down at the junction a tavern sprung up*
> *Where they served up a manlier brew*
> *And they lifted their glasses to King Alcohol*
> *And to hell with Joe Goodrich and crew*[17]

When I went to Milton College in 1953, the liquor ban was still in effect, and anyone who wanted a drink had to drive a few blocks into downtown Milton Junction and stop at one of the bars. The town park in the center of Milton remained sacrosanct. And then one day it happened: a young lawyer decided to see if there were any legal grounds for prohibiting a tavern in Milton and discovered that, like much of Goodrich's efforts, the agreement was one made on mutual trust and was never formalized. It was a matter of honor among gentlemen. When the proposal to permit the sale of alcohol in Milton came up for a vote, it passed with hardly a whimper.

> *For 126 years in the town, Joe Goodrich's will had its way*
> *There was never a tavern on Goodrich's land,*
> *though the family had long passed away*
> *And some called it progress but most didn't care*
> *When they voted the liquor ban down*
> *And not many remembered Joe Goodrich's dream*
> *When he first bought the land for the town*[18]

And so after all those years the Park View Bar was built on one of the parcels of land originally given to a merchant who swore never to drink alcohol.

And what of Goodrich's dream? He is still remembered as the founder of Milton and a great visionary, and the Milton Historical Society gives him full recognition for all he accomplished, but over at the Park View Bar, his name is rarely spoken.

> *Now down at the Park View they sit at the bar*
> *And go drifting away on the tide*
> *And there's never a mention of Goodrich's name*
> *You might think that his vision has died*
> *Now don't get me wrong, I'm no different than you*
> *I've been known to partake now and then*
> *But if you're worth your salt you'll hang on to your dreams*
> *They're still the best measure of man*[19]

Goodrich may be long gone and his name has been forgotten by many, but I don't think I could take a drink at the Park View Bar. I just don't think it would taste right.

Thinking about the conversation sitting there at that small table reminds me of the book *Fried Green Tomatoes*. Great stories never die, and in the retelling, characters long since gone spring to life. They are as real as the people you pass on the street, and our lives have all been made richer because of their dreams. Joe Goodrich's dream has not been forgotten—I was just talking about it with a stranger at the airport in Amsterdam.

BOB-BOB-BOB, BOB-BOBRA ANN

They came hungry. Word had spread throughout the countryside that there was a prophet performing miracles. Jesus had been teaching on the coasts of Tyre and Sidon and had just cast the Devil out of a woman. When he returned to the Sea of Galilee, he went up onto a mountain. Sitting there, he watched a multitude of people gathering around him.

> And great multitudes came unto him, having with them those who were lame, blind, maimed and many others, casting them down at Jesus' feet; and he healed them.
>
> (Matthew 15:30)

When Jesus looked upon the multitude of people, he had compassion on them.

> Then Jesus called his disciples unto him, and said, I have compassion on the multitude, because they continue with me three days, and have nothing to eat; and I will not send them away fasting, lest they faint in the way.
>
> (Matthew 15:32)

When he instructed his disciples to feed the crowd, they wondered at his command, as they only had a few little fishes and seven loaves of bread. They should have known that Christ would never send people home with an empty stomach. They came for spiritual nourishment, which Christ gave through his word and his healings. With just a few fishes, Christ gave them bodily nourishment as well.

> *And they did all eat, and were filled: and they took up of the broken meat that was left seven baskets full. And they that did eat were four thousand men, beside women and children.*
> (Matthew 15:37–38)

Christ still feeds the multitudes.

Last night I went to pick up a couple of fish-and-chip dinners at the local Big Y supermarket. It's the only place you can get fish and chips in the area. I've never seen more than two people in line, but last night there must have been fifteen, not counting all the people who'd placed their orders and were shopping while they waited. Maybe it was because it was a Friday night in Lent. When I got up to the counter and placed my order, they told me it would be forty-five minutes instead of the usual twenty. They had more than enough fish to feed everyone, but they only had two fryers. The four men who were frying the fish and chips must have wondered how they could feed so many people.

After picking up a few things, I came back to wait and, if anything, the crowd had gotten even larger. Standing around talking to people, I found out some of them had been waiting for over an hour. I noticed a man standing in line who'd placed his order just before I had. I'd seen him wandering around the store earlier with a small basket, half filled. When I asked him if he'd picked up his fish yet, he told me they weren't ready. Two of the people I talked to had called their orders in, and they had already been waiting for an hour and a half. It didn't take long to get to know the names of some of the folks who were standing there waiting. The man who placed his order just before mine walked over and stuck out his hand.

"My name's Leo," he said

"Glad to meet you, Leo. I'm Jerry."

It looked like we were going to be spending some time together. Leo and his wife, Nora, had never bought fish and chips there before and couldn't believe how many people were standing around waiting.

"I've gotten fish here a lot of times, and I've never seen more than two people in line," I said. "It usually doesn't take more than fifteen or twenty minutes. I didn't think about it when I came here, but I shouldn't be surprised at the crowd. It's Lent, and this is Friday. I used to be a Catholic, but I didn't make the connection."

"I grew up in the Catholic Church, and did the whole thing—altar boy and all the rest," Leo said. "It all seems like a lot of mumbo jumbo to me."

"I don't have a problem with rituals," I said. "Some people find them meaningful. If you reach the point where the rituals don't mean anything anymore, then you're just doing something because someone said you were supposed to do it."

Leo nodded in agreement. "Now I just try to live a good life and help other people whenever I can. That's enough for me."

Leo struck me as a man who lives his faith. That's what we're supposed to do.

> What doth it profit, my brethren, though a man say he hath faith, and have not works? Can faith save him? . . . Even so faith, if it hath not works is dead, being alone . . . . Ye see then how that by works a man is justified, and not by faith only.
>
> (James 2:14, 17, 24)

"I've forgotten the significance of eating fish on Fridays," I said. "From what I remember from when I was a Catholic, we were required to eat fish every Friday in Lent, but somewhere along the line they changed it to just Good Friday. Today isn't Good Friday, so maybe Lent doesn't have anything to do with it. Maybe people just didn't feel like cooking tonight, like me."

"I have a friend who is Catholic, and he says they don't eat meat on Wednesdays either, so don't come on Wednesday nights during Lent," Leo said.

Mark was standing next to us, leaning back against the frozen-fish counter. Turning to him I said, "Maybe we should just grab a fish-and-chips TV dinner."

Mark was one of the people who had called his order in early. He told me, "I called my order in an hour and a half ago, and it's still not ready!"

"Maybe they should call this the Big W-H-Y," I said, sounding out the letters individually.

Mark was a stocky man, decorated with tattoos that wound their way up his arms and all the way up his neck to his chin. Talking with him, I tried not to be too obvious as I read the tattoos on his neck. They were done in the Old English–style of typography and reminded me of the way the deacon's speech was illuminated in the old Pogo comic strips. Considering how long he'd been waiting, he seemed remarkably calm and composed. Under the circumstances, I might have expected a lot more anger in the crowd, but people seemed in good spirits. Occasionally, a new customer would come up and place their order, then spot a friend in the crowd. But for the most part, we were all strangers. Like the multitude on the mountain overlooking the Sea of Galilee, the group was made up of believers and skeptics. I don't imagine that many of them were thinking about Jesus at the moment.

As the minutes passed, the young woman behind the counter became more and more apologetic. "I have to apologize for how long you have to wait," she said.

"There's no need to apologize," I said. "I'm in good health, I have a nice car to drive, so I can come over here, and when I walk down the aisles, I can put anything I want in my cart without worrying about how I am going to pay for it. I have no reason to complain. I'm having a good time." Oddly enough, I was. Several people smiled and nodded their heads in agreement.

As each order came up, the young woman behind the counter called out the name of the customer who'd placed the order. "Bob?" she said, looking around the crowd. Nobody responded, and the kidding began.

"Tell me what the order is and I might just be Bob," someone called out, and everyone laughed.

Every three or four minutes, the woman behind the counter called out "Bob" hopefully. I laughed to myself and started singing softly, "Bob-Bob-Bob, Bob-Bobra Ann." Leo was standing next to me and had been joined by his wife, Nora. When the woman called "Lucy" to pick up the next order, I turned to Leo and said, "She must be Lucy in the sky with diamonds," and he laughed. "I can do this all night if I have to."

"As long as the woman behind the counter doesn't start singing 'Good Night, Sweetheart, Good Night,' we'll be all right," Leo said, and we both laughed.

Donna's order came up next. She was a pretty young black woman who had smiled warmly when I was kidding around, so I started singing "Oh, Donna," from the old Ritchie Valens record. She turned toward me after she picked up her order and gave me a warm smile, her precious fish and chips clutched firmly in her hand.

Jim was next. He was one of the people who'd been there almost two hours, so I knew how happy he was to hear his name. As he passed by me to pick up his prize, I said, "Jim Dandy to the rescue," and he smiled. LaVern Baker would have been pleased.

When Mark's name was called, a young man I hadn't noticed before quickly walked up to the counter, his billfold in hand. Meanwhile, the Mark who was standing next to me and had been waiting almost two hours just stood there quietly. When the young man at the counter was ready to pay for the order, Mark, who was standing next to me so patiently, walked over to the counter and said very politely, "I think that's my order." He asked the woman what was in the bag, and as soon as she told him, the young man at the counter realized it wasn't his order and stepped back rather sheepishly.

"Nice try, Phil!" I called out, and everybody laughed.

"What are you trying to do, start a riot?" Leo said, and everyone laughed, including the young Mark, who'd thought the order was his. We were all in a good mood and enjoying the fellowship, like skiers trapped in a lodge during a blizzard.

While we stood there waiting for the next order to be called out, I tried to come up with a song with the name Mark in it. Nothing came to mind, and my little game ended quietly, as my order was called.

"Hallelujah!" I shouted. I celebrated the miracle of the fish, just like the multitude that had trusted in Jesus to feed them on that mountaintop two thousand years ago.

On the way home, I tried to come up with a song with the name Mark in it. The best I could come up with was "Mark, the Herald Angel Sang," but I don't think I could have gotten away with it. Just when I stopped thinking about it, the song came to mind.

> *Matthew Mark, Luke and John*
> *All those disciples are dead and gone*
> *Keep your hand on the plow, hold on*[20]

Some people think of Jesus as someone who lived a long time ago, who has no concern for us. Christ is the Good Shepherd, and he still feeds his flock, whether they are a multitude having a mountaintop experience or a group of strangers stopping by to pick up an order of fish and chips at the Big Y.

I WON'T COMPLAIN

The cards are dealt with no explanation
You take what you're given and give it your best
But still it seems wrong that so many should suffer
When all they believe in is put to the test

CHORUS:

God bless those who find mercy in sleep
All those who sow who never will reap
All those who search who never find peace
May they find rest tonight[21]

"*L*ife isn't fair!" How many times have you heard someone say that? I wonder why people even bother to state the obvious. The song "Farther Along" talks about the confusion and frustration we feel when we see the unfairness.

> *Tempted and tried, we're oft made to wonder*
> *Why it should be thus all the day long*
> *When we see others living about us*
> *Never molested though in the wrong*[22]

While we may not understand the troubles we see around us, the song offers comfort:

> *Cheer up my brothers, live in the sunshine*
> *We'll understand it all by and by*

My wife, Ruth, and I have been blessed by the strong faith we've seen in those who have been dealt a bad hand of cards. They may not be able to live a full life because of physical limitations, but they can still praise the Lord for the blessings they've known.

One of the people we've visited for many years has multiple sclerosis. Lena has been suffering from the ravaging effects of the illness since she was a young woman and for many years has been confined to a bed. She can no longer use her hands and is completely at the mercy of those who care for her. Her life on most levels is very limited, but she has Jesus. And that makes all the difference. In recent years she's been in and out of hospitals and health care centers, and it's become increasingly difficult to keep up with all her moves. To complicate matters, we live an hour's drive away, so we can't visit her as often as we used to when we lived in the same town.

Last week we finally had a chance to visit her in a health care center. When we arrived, she wasn't in her room, so we asked the head nurse where we could find her. She directed us down the hall to the recreation room, and when we went in, we were faced with several rows of patients in wheelchairs lined up in front of a large-screen television. When we walked up behind her and came into her line of sight, her face lit up with a radiant smile.

"Oh, my God!" she cried out, grinning from ear to ear.

That is always her greeting when we visit her. It's more than an expression. Her joy at seeing us is all a part of her love for God, and he is present with her at all times. It's almost as if she is turning to God and saying, "Look who's here!"

Whenever we ask her, "How are you doing?" she answers, "I'm fine. I can't complain."

Something is going on here. By most people's definitions, Lena is far from "fine." But she is in a state of grace that brings peace to her days. She's not the only one. Many of the people we visit who are crippled and confined to wheelchairs or beds are doing "just fine" too. They find their comfort in the cross.

> *When in affliction's valley I tread the road of care*
> *My Savior helps me carry the cross so heavy to bear*
> *Tho' all around me is darkness and earthly joys are flown*
> *My Savior whispers his promise, never to leave me alone*[23]

Christ never promised an easy life for those who follow him. He promised that he'd give us rest.

> Come unto me, all ye that labor and are heavy laden, and I will give you rest. Take my yoke upon you, and learn of me: for I am meek and lowly in heart; and ye shall find rest unto your souls. For my yoke is easy, and my burden is light.
> (Matthew 11:28–30)

When Christ is there beside you, he will give you rest. And you won't complain.

HIS EYE IS ON THE SPARROW

Joy to the world the Lord is come! Let earth receive her king
Let ev'ry heart prepare him room
And heav'n and nature sing, and heav'n and nature sing
And heav'n and heav'n and nature sing[24]

*N*ature sings. The whole earth rejoices in the goodness of the Lord. It is no surprise that people play the sounds from nature to calm their hearts and give them rest. Nature has been the inspiration for many great symphonies and works of art. Judy Garland sang longingly out of the desire of her heart to fly over the rainbow, and in the process won the hearts of millions of people.

King David expressed his longing to dwell in the courts of the Lord, envying the lowly sparrows and swallows that made their homes in its altars.

> *My soul longeth, yea, even fainteth for the courts of the Lord: my heart and my flesh crieth out to the living God. Yea, the sparrow hath found a house, and the swallow a nest for herself, where she may lay her young, even thine altars.*
>
> (Psalm 84:2–3)

The Lord tested Elijah's faith by sending him into a ravine where there was no food. God sent some unlikely friends to minister to Elijah.

And the word of the Lord came unto him saying, Get thee hence, and turn thee eastward, and hide thyself by the brook Cherith that is before Jordan. And it shall be, that thou shalt drink of the brook; and I have commanded the ravens to feed thee there. So he went and did according unto the word of the Lord, for he went and dwelt by the brook Cherith, that is before Jordan.

(1 Kings 17:2–6)

Sometimes a ram in the bush is a raven.

Like the lilies of the field, birds have always been admired for their beauty and for their freedom, not being tied to the ground like mortal man. They soar to heights not imagined at the time of Christ. Maya Angelou wrote of freed birds and why they sing in *I know Why the Caged Bird Sings*.

Nature holds a wonder that far surpasses anything that science can teach us. And as often happens, the beauty of God's creation is best seen through the eyes of a child.

It was a beautiful early summer morning, and the kids came tumbling into the room sparking energy like a downed power line. I was teaching a nature class for five-year-olds at the museum and nature center where I was working, and I'd promised the kids that I'd take them on a trip out to the swamp. They'd been looking forward to it and were raring to go.

"Are we going out to the swamp today, Mister Razznewton?" one of the kids asked. Some of the kids had trouble wrapping their tongue around my name.

"We sure are!" I answered. "Before we go out, though, I want everyone to settle down for a minute. You're not going to see anything if you're this noisy!

"Today we're going to talk about bird songs, and when we get out to the swamp, if you're completely quiet and cut out the wiggling, I'll try to call a bird and get him to come to us. Does anyone know why birds sing?"

"Because they're happy?" one of the kids asked hesitantly.

"No," I answered. "Most of the time, they're saying 'This is my place, and if you've got any ideas about moving in on my territory, you're in for a fight!'"

When the kids started laughing I asked them, "If some strange kid came into your yard and started messing around with your bike, wouldn't you start yelling at him to get out of your yard?"

They chimed in, "Sure!"

"Well, that's what birds do. And when you hear a bird singing, it's a male. The females are the quiet ones." The little girls liked that. "The other reason why male birds sing is to attract females. They like to sit up on a high branch with the sun shining on their breast and sing at the top of their little bird lungs. They are a lot like rock singers. If they hear another bird singing, they're going to investigate, and if the bird is on their property, there's going to be a fight." I had gotten the kids' attention, and they sat quietly, waiting for the moment when we'd head out to the swamp.

It was a five-minute walk through the woods to the swamp, and the kids were uncharacteristically quiet. Most people, when they go for a walk in the woods, talk a blue streak and make so much noise that the woods seem dead to them. On this day, we walked in silence, and the woods seemed alive with sounds and smells. We were like explorers set out to discover a familiar world.

As we walked along, I quietly rehearsed what we were going to do. We'd sit on a log from a fallen tree that was camouflaged by spice bushes. Sitting there, we'd be hidden but still able to look out onto the swamp. Once we were settled down and completely quiet, I'd try to call a bird to us. I'd done this many times when I sat on that log eating lunch. I'd been successful in calling a bird over to within a few feet of me, but I hadn't had ten wiggly five-year-olds sitting next to me on the log.

After we'd settled in, the kids sat quietly as we listened for a bird call. We didn't have to wait long. A song sparrow called out his chirrupy song from across the small swamp, and he went unchallenged until I answered him with my best song sparrow imitation. We sat there waiting, to see if I'd get a response. Sure enough, after a brief pause, he called again, this time sounding a little closer. Each time he'd call, I'd answer him, and each time he'd moved closer until we finally could see him. Somewhere along the way, the kids had stopped breathing.

Finally, he flew over toward us and sat on a branch no more than six feet away from us, just over our heads. He fluffed his feathers, stuck out his chest, and let out his most ferocious call, glaring down at me. I answered him right back. He seemed a little confused by then. He'd never seen a song sparrow like me, and he was not impressed with my singing. He gave one more defiant call, and sat there with a self-satisfied air, as I made a feeble attempt to imitate him.

Meanwhile, the kids were about to pass out from holding their breath. When it became obvious to mister song sparrow that I was no threat to him as a singer, or a potential suitor for his mate, he turned around, flipped up his little tail dismissively, and flew off. A couple of minutes later he was back at his old post, singing out a warning. Finally, I told the kids it was all right to breathe. It was time to head back to the nature center, but no one wanted to leave. They were still mesmerized by the experience.

Walking back through the woods, a little girl walked beside me, lost in the moment. Looking up at me, she said wistfully, "Mister Rasmussen, I could stay out in the woods with you forever."

Thinking back on all that I had said about why birds sing, I felt that I had missed something. I know that birds sing to protect their territory. All wild animals stake out their turf. Dogs do it by hosing down every tree and fence post in sight. Birds' bladders are too small for that, so they sing. Many animals besides birds use bright colors to attract a mate. But there's more than that. Birds sing the sun up every morning. I've never heard a valid scientific explanation for that. The little boy who hesitantly answered my first question by saying that birds sing because they are happy may have the best explanation. All heaven and nature sing at the goodness of God.

> *I sing because I'm happy*
> *I sing because I'm free*
> *His eye is on the sparrow*
> *And I know he watches me*[25]

I have the feeling that God was sitting on the end of that log, watching us. I bet He had a wonderful time.

MEOLOGY

"*If God is so loving, why does he allow suffering?*"
That's one of the favorite questions posed by atheists, prefaced with a silent, "Oh, yeah?" For someone out to prove that God doesn't exist, it's most likely a losing battle trying to give an answer they would accept. The best response I could give is to recommend reading Harold Kushner's book When Bad Things Happen to Good People. Kushner's son died at the age of fourteen, and it was a question he had to grapple with. I'd rather approach the question from another direction.

You want to talk about suffering? Can you imagine the pain that God experienced, knowingly sending his only begotten son to earth to die one of the most excruciatingly painful deaths man has ever devised? Worse than that, Christ was completely innocent and died for OUR sins. God has willingly suffered the greatest pain out of love for us.

And what about Jesus? Nothing can equal the suffering he bore on the cross, but then, his life was filled with suffering. Jesus, in mourning for Jerusalem, expressed his sorrow eloquently.

> *O Jerusalem, Jerusalem, thou that killest the prophets, and stonest them which are sent unto thee, how often would I have gathered thy children together, even as a hen gathereth her chickens under her wings, and ye would not.*
>
> (Matthew 23:37)

You can hear the heartache in Christ's voice. As Christ observed, "A prophet is not without honor, save in his own country, and in his own house" (Matthew 13:57).

When we sin, we sin against God, and it hurts him. We should understand that well, especially if we have been blessed with children. When they do something destructive, we often suffer for it more than they do, at least in the short term. When they reject God, it causes us great pain. That's how God feels when we reject him or go against his will.

There's a wonderful old gospel song called How Much Do I Owe Him? *When it was recorded by the Swanee Quintet, it was a time when records were limited to three minutes in length, so there were only two verses.*

> *They led my Savior up that hill*
> *They whipped him all night long*
> *They took a sword and pierced his side*
> *He hung his head and he died*
>
> CHORUS:
>
> *How much do I owe him? How much do I owe him?*
> *How much do I owe him? He died just for me*
>
> *There were two thieves hung beside him*
> *One said, Lord remember me*
> *And when you walk into your father's house*
> *Remember me in paradise*

I felt limited because the song was so short, so I wrote another verse.

> *When I look down in my heart*
> *And see all that I see*
> *You know, it makes me stop and wonder*
> *Why Christ would die for me*

Instead of asking why God should allow us to suffer, we should ask why we cause him to suffer, and why he still loves us, anyway.

If I ever wonder how much God loves me, I think of all the prayers of mine he has answered. I know that he is a prayer-answering God. At the same time, I praise his holy name for the prayers he didn't answer. Looking back, I realize I would have been in serious trouble if he had answered them. Prayer is a funny thing. We ask God for things with the greatest confidence, forgetting that he knows what's good for us, much more than we do. Besides, if we really want to do his will, we should ask him to guide us in his way. Our lives would be so much better if we would only pray like Jesus: "Not my will, but thine be done" (John 22:42).

He doesn't need any suggestions about how he should do his job. When we don't do his will, there are consequences.

"Whom the Lord loves, he chasteneth" (Hebrews 12:6). *Chasteneth* is not a word we use much. I had to look it up to make sure I really knew the definition. I think of someone who has been chastened as someone who has been admonished. That's nowhere near the actual meaning of the word. Merriam-Webster's first definition is much stronger: To chasten is to "correct by punishment or suffering."

Like every gift from God, prayer can be misused. Speaking for me, much of the suffering I've experienced in life was because I didn't get prayer right. And when you get things wrong, God chastens you, out of love. These days, I see prayer appearing in all guises. Last night, a program came on TV with a preacher hawking his book on "Prosperity Thinking." He's selling prayer as a way to get stuff. I do believe in the power of prayer, and I believe miracles still happen. The danger is that we can fall into the trap where we look at God as existing to fulfill our desires. And too often, you have to buy somebody's book if you really want to have your prayers answered. The preacher I was listening to last night has his own twist. If you get his book, and follow his instructions to the letter, you can pray for a specific dollar amount and get it. One satisfied customer asked for $12,000 and got it, to the penny! Part of the methodology of the preacher's system is that you need to buy bottles of his Miracle Spring Water: God in a bottle. I wonder if there is a five-cent deposit on it. After all, God has always been in favor of redemption.

Most of us have a more mature approach to prayer, but our selfishness can rear its ugly head without our even realizing it. There's always the danger that our theology becomes "meology." When we become too focused on what we want from the Lord and don't trust the Lord enough to let him order our steps, we pay for it somewhere down the line.

> *I wake up every morning to start another day*
> *I ask the Lord to place my feet on the narrow way*
> *There's trouble all around me as far as I can see*
> *But that's all right, I don't mind, He's working on me*
>
> CHORUS:
>
> *He's working on me, he's working on me*
> *And though I may not be the man I ought to be*
> *In all I do and all I say, I ask the Lord to show the way*
> *Brother can't you see, he's working on me*[26]

Just as God rejoices when we do his will, he is pained when we reject him to satisfy our own selfish desires. If we place God's will at the center of our worship, he will show us his way.

In prayer, our wish should be that our importance be decreased, while God's is increased. John the Baptist said of Jesus, "He must increase, but I must decrease" (John 3:30).

Theology is the study of God. There's no "me" in theology.

CUTOUTS

There's a little black train a' coming
Better get your business right
There's a little black train a' coming
And it may be here tonight[27]

Death has become a growth industry. Or, at least the anticipation of death has. Instead of being concerned about getting your business right, people are encouraged to squeeze every ounce of self-gratification, excitement, and pleasure out of their life while they can. When the prospect of approaching death becomes a reality, rather than spending their remaining days in reflection and repentance, people are encouraged to make a "bucket list" of all the experiences they want to have before they "kick the bucket." When I turn on my computer, there's an advertisement on my home screen for "365 things to do on Long Island before you die."

Terminal illnesses are good for tourism. There was even a popular movie with Jack Nicholson and Morgan Freeman entitled The Bucket List. There's something a little sad about the whole concept. If you have been told you only have a short time to live, why would you want to spend it racing around the country trying to cram as many exciting experiences into your life as you could? It sounds desperate to me. For *a Christian, there's nothing you can do on earth that can compare to the glories of heaven, anyway.*

We all have places and experiences we'd like to have the opportunity to enjoy. There's nothing wrong with taking that trip to see the Grand Canyon, if you've wanted to go there all your life. But, if you don't have your house in order, you'd better make that your first priority. Sooner or later, we will all be called upon to give an accounting for our lives. We wouldn't want to face Saint Peter like Bill Jones does in this story:

Bill Jones had a life that many people would envy. He'd been a very successful businessman. The long hours he'd worked that kept him away from his wife and children were compensated for by the occasional affairs he'd had at the office. On the whole, he thought he'd been a pretty good person. When his doctor told him he had six months to live, he was stunned. The first thing he thought of was all the things he'd never had a chance to do because he'd been too busy working. When he first heard about making a bucket list, he found the idea offensive, but the more he thought about it, the better it sounded. Why shouldn't he have a good time? After all, he'd earned it.

He'd always wanted to try skydiving, so he made arrangements to go up in a plane at the local airport and try his hand at jumping out of an airplane, to see what it felt like to be freefalling in space, waiting until the last moment to pull the parachute cord. From that moment on, every day was spent experiencing new pleasures. Why hadn't he thought of this earlier?

When Bill finally died, he had his case all laid out for Saint Peter. He'd lived a pretty good life. Yes, he'd slipped a little, once in a while, but doesn't everyone? Just considering the good things he'd done, he thought he'd earned his way into heaven. When Bill met Saint Peter at the pearly gates, he wasn't expecting the response he got from Saint Peter. He didn't think Peter would bring up his skydiving or all the things he'd checked off his bucket list, one by one. He had just been having a good time while he still could.

"Was that he best way you could think of to live the last days of your life?" Saint Peter asked. "I suppose it's not surprising, because you spent your whole life thinking about yourself."

"What did you expect me to do?" Bill responded. "Is there anything wrong with having a good time?"

Peter had heard that argument more times than he cared to remember. "Did you ever read the Bible?" Peter asked. "Christ made it very clear we are to live our lives helping others." And then Peter recited the lines from Saint Matthew as he'd done countless times before:

> And the King shall answer and say unto them, Verily I say unto you, Inasmuch as ye have done it unto one of the least of these my brethren, ye have done it unto me. . . .Then shall he say unto them on the left hand, Depart from me, ye cursed, into everlasting fire, prepared for the devil and his angels. For I was a hungered, and ye gave me no meat; I was thirsty and, an ye gave me no drink; I was a stranger, and ye took me not in; naked and ye clothed me not. . . .In as much as ye did it not to one of the least of my brethren, ye did it not to me.
> (Matthew 25:40, 42–43, 45)

"You should have spent your days helping others, rather than just satisfying your own desires," Peter said.

Bill looked completely defeated. He could see he wasn't going to be able to talk his way out of this one.

Saint Peter had had enough, and there was a long line of people waiting behind Bill. "You'll find the Down elevator on the other side of that cloud," Peter said, waving his hand dismissively. "When you get in, just press the Hell button."

He was standing next to a large bin of five-dollar DVDs at the Wal-Mart store. When I walked up to the display, he was so intent upon searching through the pile of DVDs, he didn't notice me. I was killing time, waiting for my wife to do her shopping, and I didn't expect to find anything in the bin. I'd looked through similar piles of cutout DVDs many times and had almost exhausted any potential for finding something I wanted. Five dollars isn't a bargain for a movie you're not interested in seeing. When he looked up and noticed me, he smiled and said, "I love DVDs!"

"Me too," I said, returning his smile. He was a short man, not much taller than the display bin, with a touch of white hair in his temples.

"I have so many DVDs I don't even know what I have anymore. I just keep buying them. Sometimes I have to get a cart just to carry them, I buy so many."

"I don't find much I want to buy anymore," I said. "I've already got most of the DVDs I want to see. Sometimes, though, I run across something I haven't seen that looks interesting, and for five dollars you can't go wrong."

Both of us went back to our rummaging through the haphazardly dumped pile of DVDs, hoping to find something we wanted. It wasn't that there weren't any good movies in the pile. There were quite a few I already owned. There just weren't any that caught my fancy, and I knew my wife would be done shopping soon.

"Have you seen this one?" I asked, holding up Stanley Kubrick's *The Shining*. "I waited a long time for this one to come down in price enough so that I could buy it, and here it is for five dollars." The man reached over to take it and said, "I think I might already have this, but I'll take it anyway."

"If you do have it, you can always pass it on to someone who doesn't," I said. "I do that all the time."

"I'll never have enough time to watch all the movies I already have, anyway" the man said with a resigned tone in his voice. "I'm just fifty-two years old and I have cancer. I don't know how much longer I have to live." Suddenly, the aimless sifting through old DVDs took on an entirely different feeling.

"Oh, I'm really sorry to hear that," I said. "That has to be terribly hard to deal with."

"I'm just trying to enjoy whatever days I still have left," he said.

I thought about the conversation I'd had with my wife as we were walking into the store. In the last month, I've received good reports from all of my annual checkups. My optometrist gave me a clean bill of health on my eyes, and I'd just gotten equally good reports from my general practitioner and two other doctors. I was feeling extremely thankful and blessed. For a moment, the thought crossed my mind to tell the man how blessed I was to have good health, but the Lord stilled my tongue.

For a couple of minutes neither of us said a word. We both kept searching through the DVDs, but that wasn't where my mind was. I finally spotted a movie that looked interesting. By then, the man had five or six movies and was still looking for more.

"Well, I have to be on my way, now," I said. "My wife may be done shopping, and I don't want to keep her waiting. I'll keep you in prayer." I had no way of knowing whether being kept in prayer would mean anything to the man, but he seemed so alone, and I didn't know if he had anyone to pray for him. Most people appreciate that you care enough about them to remember them in prayer, even if they don't believe in God.

"Take care of yourself, now," I said, and turned my shopping cart to move away from the DVD bin. He gave me a wan smile as if to say "thank you," and said something too softly for me to hear. Looking back, I could see that he was still intently looking through the display bin.

My heart is still heavy, thinking of that man at Wal-Mart, filling his time searching through cutout DVDs. He's probably never heard of making a bucket list. If he has, he's got to be the only person who has buying five-dollar DVDs from the cutout bin at Wal-Mart on his list.

There will come a time for each of us when that little black train will pull into the station. May we live our lives as if that day were today.

THE ELEVENTH COMMANDMENT

Maybe Moses started it. He gave us the first "Top Ten" list. Then there were the Seven Wonders of the World, and more recently, the New Seven Wonders of the World. Everybody loves lists. When I was a kid growing up in the 'forties, we all gathered around the radio every week to see what the top ten songs were on Your Hit Parade. I don't think I ever missed a program. Every week when the new Hit Parade magazine came out, I'd stop by Star Billiards and plunk down my dime to get the lyrics to all the top songs of the week. I still remember the lyrics to many of those songs.

> And the three mile creek was four miles long, back when I was young
> And I knew the words to every song known to the human tongue[28]

In recent years they've elevated the top-ten list to absurd levels. I'm sure that Moses would be horrified if he turned on the television and watched The Ten Most Outrageous Bathrooms. What has the world come to? If Moses were on TV, they'd chop up the Ten Commandments into groups of two or three so that they could fit commercials between them and build suspense. "We'll be right back after these messages. Stay tuned to find out which commandment is going to be NUMBER ONE." Of course, God never presented the Ten Commandments in any particular order. Once you got past the first two, which Christ said *were the most important, you could put them in any order you want. It just wouldn't make good television.*

When it comes to lists, the runners-up don't carry a lot of weight. How many people remember that King Kong was the "Eighth Wonder of the World"? It's anybody's guess what might have been the eleventh commandment if God had chosen to make one. If all the major theologians got together, they could have a contest to decide what should be the eleventh commandment. And then they could televise the results.

He arrived just as we were getting in line for the buffet dinner. Each Wednesday during the Lenten season one of the churches in Shelton hosted a buffet dinner, followed by a service. My wife and I were already in line for the dinner when he arrived. He stepped in behind me, and as we approached the table, and we exchanged a quick, "Hello, how're you doin'?" He was a tall, thin young man all dressed in black, and my first thought was that he was a minister, although he wasn't wearing a collar. My wife, Ruth, and I had missed the first two Wednesday night services, and I asked him if he'd made them. He answered, "I made one of them," just as we got to the buffet tables, and then all conversation stopped. Food does that.

When Ruth and I had been invited to come to the service, my friend Pastor Ken Smith of First Baptist Church asked me if I would do a song about Jonah, as the guest minister would be preaching a sermon about him. Like Noah, Jonah is one of those Bible characters that lend themselves to song, and I had written three songs with verses about Jonah. The one I chose to do takes a rather humorous approach to the story, as most songs do.

> *God sent Jonah across the sea in the belly of a whale*
> *He sent him on down to Nineveh, and he lived to tell the tale*
> *He told them people better mind your ways,*
> *you better get ready for the judgment day*
> *And just because you like to do it, that don't make it right*[29]

After dinner, we headed upstairs to the sanctuary for the service. I noticed that the man in black sat in the front row next to Ken and had put on a minister's collar. He was the preacher who was going to give the night's sermon. After the praise-and-worship songs, Pastor Ken introduced me, and I went up and did my song. When I finished the song, he told a humorous story and then introduced the preacher for the night, Reverend Timothy Hare, the man in black.

The story of Jonah is pretty straightforward. God tells Jonah to warn the people of Nineveh. Jonah refuses and skips town on a boat. God gets angry and has a whale swallow Jonah. After three days, the whale has had enough of Jonah and spits him onto shore near Nineveh. Jonah tells the people of Nineveh to shape up or ship out. End of story. There are several obvious messages that Reverend Hare could have given: Don't get God angry, or there's no telling what he might do to you; don't live a sinful life like the people of Nineveh; God is a forgiving God. Or, you can take the story at face value. The problem with that is it only leads to arguments about whether a man could survive for three days in the belly of a whale. We're not talking Geppetto here.

Before we get to Reverend Hare's comments, perhaps it would be good to refresh our memory about the story. We'll pick it up after Jonah reluctantly delivered the message from God to the people of Nineveh.

> And God saw their works, that they turned from their evil way; and God repented of the evil, that he had said he would do unto them; and he did it not . . . . But it displeased Jonah exceedingly, and he was very angry . . . . Therefore now O Lord, take, I beseech thee, my life from me; for it is better for me to die than to live.
> (Jonah 3:10; 4:1, 3)

Jonah was *really* angry. He went outside of the city and made a little booth where he could sit and watch what God was going to do. God saw him sitting out there in the blazing sun and prepared a gourd to cast a shadow over his head. The next day, seeing no change in Jonah, God prepared a worm that smote the gourd to the ground.

> And God said to Jonah, Doest thou well to be angry for the gourd? And he said, I do well to be angry, even unto death. Then said the

> Lord, Thou hast had pity on the gourd, for the which thou has not labored, neither madest it grow; which came up in a night and perished in the night.
>
> (Jonah 4:9–10)

You would think that Jonah would be thankful. After all, God had delivered him from the belly of the whale. It would have been wise not to get God angry now that Jonah was safely on dry land. He certainly didn't want to get swallowed again. Jonah wasn't thinking about that. He was angry that God forgave the people of Nineveh. He had every reason to feel blessed, but he was burning with anger. God had forgiven him for his sins, and yet he was determined to remain angry. Nobody likes a poor winner.

God tried to reason with Jonah.

> And should not I spare Nineveh, that great city, wherein are more than six score thousand persons that cannot discern between their right hand and their left hand, and also much cattle?
>
> (Jonah 4:11)

And that's how the book ends. We are left with many questions. We never know whether Jonah saw the wisdom in God's question and let go of his anger. As far as we know, he was never swallowed by a whale again.

Reverend Hare's sermon dealt with two issues. If people question how Jonah could have survived in the belly of a whale, as Reverend Hare said, it seems even more unbelievable that every person in Nineveh repented and wore sackcloth and sat in ashes, including the king. As the book says:

> So the people of Nineveh believed God, and proclaimed a fast, and put on sackcloth, from the greatest of them even to the least of them.
>
> (Jonah 3:5)

The point that Reverend Hare made that resonated most strongly with me was how bitter and unforgiving Jonah was. Even though God forgave him for being openly disobedient, Jonah could not forgive the people of Nineveh. Sometimes our emotions overrule our reason. How many times have we harbored anger and resentment toward others, like Jonah, refusing to let go of those bad feelings? Jonah wanted the people of Nineveh to be punished, even though God had forgiven him. I suppose he wondered why they should get away with what they'd done, now that he had become so righteous.

> *Tempted and tried we're oft made to wonder*
> *Why it should be thus all the day long*
> *While there are others living about us*
> *Never molested, though in the wrong*[30]

Jesus had a lot to say about forgiveness and judging others. In the Sermon on the Mount, Christ gave fair warning.

> Judge not, that ye be not judged. For with what judgment ye judge ye shall be judged; and with what measure ye mete, it shall be measured to you again. And why beholdest thou the mote that is in thy brother's eye, but considerest not the beam that is in thine own eye?
>
> (Matthew 7:1–3)

In his anger toward the people of Nineveh, Jonah lost sight of the mote in his own eye. And the apostle Paul taught that if we have anger toward someone, we need to resolve it before the day is over (Ephesians 4:26). Jonah thought that he would do well to stay angry, even unto his death.

In Luke, there is a very telling passage where Jesus speaks about self-righteousness.

> Two men went up into the temple to pray; the one a Pharisee and the other a publican. The Pharisee stood and prayed thus with himself. God, I thank thee that I am not as other men are, extortioners, unjust, adulterers or even as this publican. I fast twice in a week, I give tithes of all I possess. And the publican standing far off, would not lift up so much as his eyes unto heaven, but smote upon his breast, saying God be merciful to me a sinner. I tell you this man went down to his house justified

rather than the other; for every one that exalteth himself shall be abased; and he that humbleth himself shall be exalteth.
(Luke 18:10–14)

There's something satisfying about reading these stories in the Bible. We easily identify with the humble publican and see the hardness of Jonah's heart. Certainly, we have nothing in common with the Pharisees. What is more difficult to see is the mote in our own eye. There is a little of the Pharisee in each of us, and like Jonah we are often less forgiving of others than God is. We all suffer from the "at least" mentality: At least I don't commit adultery, or at least I'm not an alcoholic. God doesn't call us to be "at least." He calls us to be pure of heart.

Christ put it very simply: "Be ye therefore perfect, even as your Father which is in heaven is perfect (Matthew 5:48)." Certainly, we are not to begrudge God's forgiveness of others. We need all the forgiveness we can get.

So, what is the eleventh commandment? There isn't one. But if they put it to a vote, I'd cast my lot with "Thou shalt not judge." We all need to be reminded of that. I know I do.

A RAM IN THE BUSH

"*The Lord always has a ram in the bush.*"

I've heard that phrase many times over the years, but I wasn't sure where it came from. Rams in bushes come in all sizes and shapes. In the old cowboy movies, the "ram" was the US Cavalry. When the homesteaders were barricaded in their little frontier cabin surrounded by Indians, just when it seemed like nothing could save them, you'd hear a bugle call and the sound of thundering hoofs. You knew the US Cavalry was on the way and that they'd be saved. As Christians, we are saved by Calvary, not the cavalry.

Not all rams appear at the sound of a bugle. It may not be until much later that you realize that the Lord has placed a ram in your path, to help you. Your ram may have been there all the time. It might even live next door to you.

The term "ram in a bush" comes from Genesis, in one of the most powerful stories ever told. God tested Abraham by asking him to do something that was abhorrent to him. Abraham obeyed God despite his heaviness of heart. He didn't know about the ram.

> *And it came to pass after these things, that God did tempt Abraham, and said unto him, Abraham; and he said, Behold, here I am. And he said, Take now thy son, thine only son Isaac, whom thou lovest,*

and get thee into the land of Moriah; and offer him there for a burnt offering upon one of the mountains which I tell thee of.
(Genesis 22:1–2)

Abraham called his son to him and told him that they were going up into the mountains to make a burnt offering to God. Isaac trusted his father and was obedient to his will. When Abraham and Isaac arrived at the appointed place, Isaac spoke to his father.

And Isaac spoke unto Abraham his father, and said, my father, and he said, Here am I, my son. And he said, Behold the fire and the wood; but where is the lamb for the burnt offering? And Abraham said, My son, God will provide himself a lamb for a burnt offering; so they went both of them together. And they came to the place which God had told him of, and Abraham built an altar there, and laid the wood in order, and bound Isaac his son, and laid him on the altar upon the wood. (verses 7–9)

Abraham was willing to make one of the greatest sacrifices a father can make: the life of his only son. Many years later, God would make that same decision, and Jesus would be the lamb sacrificed in payment for our sins. God never asks us to do something he isn't willing to do.

And Abraham stretched forth his hand, and took the knife to slay his son. And the angel of the Lord called unto him out of heaven and said, Abraham, Abraham; and he said, here am I. And he said, Lay not thine hand upon the lad, neither do thou anything unto him; for now I know that thou fearest God, seeing thou hast not withheld thy son, thine only son from me. And Abraham lifted up his eyes, and looked, and behold behind him a ram caught in a thicket by his horns; and Abraham went up and took the ram, and offered him up for a burnt offering in the stead of his son. (verses 10–13)

God did not desert Abraham in his time of trial. He had a ram in the bush.

The summer sun was hanging low in the sky, and the air was hot and heavy. It was no day to be outside. She was sitting on a rock in the front yard across the street from our house when I took out the garbage. When I glanced over at her, at first I thought it was Lois, who lives in the house across the street. She was about the same size and age, so I figured that Lois was waiting for a friend to pick her up. Still, it seemed odd that Lois hadn't called out a hello, because she is a very friendly woman. For the moment I was concentrating on the business at hand, lugging the garbage cans and recycling bin to the curb. I had just finished when I noticed a man who was walking his dog had stopped to talk to the woman. By that time, she'd stood up, and I saw she had a cane, so I knew it wasn't Lois.

"Can I help you?" I called over.

She answered, but I couldn't make out what she was saying because at that moment a car drove by. By then the man and his dog had gone on their way. They were concentrating on their business at hand too. When I walked over to her, I asked her again, "Can I help you?"

"I'm walking over to my sister's, but I guess it's farther away than I thought."

"Can I give you a ride?"

At first she declined. "Oh, no, I'll be all right. I just got tired."

When I asked her where her sister lived, she said, "Wakelee Avenue." I couldn't place where Wakelee Avenue was. "I'm halfway there, and I didn't know if I should go the rest of the way, or turn around and go home," she said. "It's just too hot." The woman looked like she was well up in her eighties, so I knew she couldn't have walked very far in the heat, using a cane. I knew I'd been on Wakelee Avenue, but when I thought about the names of the streets in our neighborhood, I was sure it wasn't one of them.

"Where is Wakelee Avenue?" I asked.

"You just go down the steep hill," she answered.

"We're on the top of a hill," I said. (Our house is on the highest point of Hillcrest Avenue.) "You have to go down a steep hill, any way you go."

I asked her what the name of the street was that she was talking about and she didn't know. She insisted that she could show me how to get there, so I helped her into the car and we headed down the street, looking for the steep hill. At first I followed her directions, and we ended up going in a circle and came right back to the rock she'd been sitting on. The next time we tried, I took her down one of the streets that goes down a steep hill.

"I think this is it," she said.

I wasn't convinced. I mentioned a couple of major landmarks at the bottom of the hill, and she didn't seem to know what I was talking about, so halfway down the hill I turned the car around and headed back to my house. I figured my wife would be wondering why it was taking me so long to take out the garbage. When I parked the car and turned off the motor, I told the woman, "I'm just going in to let my wife know that I'm taking you to your sister's."

When I got back into the car, I spotted a man who lives in our neighborhood out for his evening walk, so I rolled down my window and called over to him, "Do you know where Wakelee Avenue is?"

"Yeah. Turn right at the corner and head down Sentinel Hill, and then go on to Academy Hill."

"Oh, okay," I said. And then I remembered where Wakelee Avenue was. I'd driven on it many times. I didn't make the connection because, from the way the woman talked, I figured it was in our neighborhood. It's not even in the town we live in.

"It's up by Griffin Hospital, right? I turn right at the traffic light by the cemetery."

"That's it," he said.

No wonder I was confused. The woman told me that she was halfway to her sister's house, and she had only walked three blocks. Wakelee Avenue was a good three miles away.

"How did you ever think you could walk all the way to Wakelee Avenue?" I asked her.

"It was a lot shorter in my mind," she said.

As we were driving down the hill, I asked her if she recognized where we were, and she nodded her head. By the time we got down to the stop sign at the bottom of the hill, she knew where she was, and so did I.

"Do you know if your sister is home?" I asked, hopeful.

"Her husband owns a store and it's always open on Fridays, so she'll be home," she said. And then added, "Oh, this isn't Friday, is it?"

"No, it's Wednesday," I said. "We might as well go over there, as long as we've come this far. If she isn't home, then I'll take you to your house—if you can tell me how to get there." By now, I wasn't certain she could.

When we got to Wakelee Avenue, she said, "We just have to go to Westfield Avenue."

"I thought you said she lives on Wakelee Avenue."

"No, she lives on Westfield Avenue. It's right off Wakelee."

By then I wasn't sure we'd ever find the house, but she showed me where to turn to get to Westfield Avenue, and when we reached the corner, her sister's house was directly in front of us. I pulled my car into the driveway and commented that there was a light on in the living room, and I noticed their garbage had already been put out by the curb. At first, she told me not to bother getting out of the car. She'd be fine.

"There's no way I'm just going to drop you off here," I said. "They may just have left a light on, and I don't want you to be sitting on their front step until they get home." By now, it was dark out.

I got out of the car and helped her out. By the time we got to the front door, she'd changed her mind.

"Let's go," she said. "You can just take me home."

"Don't you want to ring the doorbell?" I asked.

"They aren't home. If they were, their car would be in the driveway."

There had been no car in the driveway when she told me to turn in and park, so her sudden decision not to ring the doorbell made no sense at all. By then, I just wanted to get her safely somewhere.

"Are you sure you know how to get home? If we can't find your house, I don't know what I'll do with you," I said, laughing.

Once again, I helped her into the car, and we headed back the way we had come: down a big hill. We live in a river valley, so you can't go anywhere without going down a big hill.

"My husband's dead," she said, "and my sons get very angry with me for doing things like this."

It sounded to me like this wasn't the first time she'd gone off somewhere on her own and become confused. "Don't worry about that," I said. "I don't know your sons, so I won't tell on you."

Then it occurred to me why she'd decided not to ring her sister's doorbell. She would have had to explain how she'd gotten over there, and who I was. There would have been hell to pay. She was a sweet woman, and I was glad that she decided to turn around and go home.

Driving back, the woman told me to go a different route than the one we'd taken to go to her sister's house. I had to trust that she knew what she was doing. At the top of the hill she told me where to turn onto her street. When we reached her house, I pulled my car into the driveway.

"You can just let me off here," she said.

The house was dark, but there were two cars parked in the driveway. "Whose cars are those?" I asked.

"They're my son and daughter-in-law's."

The house was dark, so I wondered why the cars were there.

"I just want to walk you to the door to make sure you get in all right," I said. I had no more intention of leaving her there without seeing that she could get in the house than I did when she wanted me to drop her off at her sister's.

"Oh, I'll be all right," she said.

"I'm just going to sit here in my car until I see you open the front door."

As she was getting out of the car, she turned to me and said, "How can I ever thank you?"

"Hey, that's what we're here for—to help each other. The Lord sent me out with our garbage just at the time you were too tired to walk any further. He knew you needed someone to help you, so he sent me. It was my pleasure."

"I don't know how I can ever repay you," she said.

"That's easy," I said. "Just give me a big smile."

And her face lit up. That was thanks enough.

I waited until I saw she'd unlocked the door, and she turned around and called out to me. I couldn't understand what she was saying, but I called back, "Have a good night, and take care of yourself!" I had a four-block ride home.

Sometimes we need a ram in the bush. Sometimes we are the ram.

A HOOF NOTE

Some days are devoured by errands. I'd just left Banko's music store after looking for a guitar strap and decided to drop in at my barber's to see if she had any space still left open for Saturday so I could get a haircut. When I walked through the doorway, I spotted Patty in the back of the shop doing a woman's hair.

"Hi, Jer!" Patty called out. "What are you up to today?"

"Not much. I just thought as long as I was in the neighborhood, I'd stop by and see if you have any time tomorrow to cut my hair."

Patty laughed and said, "No, I'm really jammed up tomorrow."

I hadn't really expected that she'd have the time because tomorrow was Saturday.

As I was talking to Patty, I realized that I knew the woman who was sitting in the chair. It was the woman I'd seen sitting on the rock across the street from our house, just three or four days before. She was sitting in the same position as she'd been on the rock, with her cane angled across her outstretched legs.

I looked down at the woman and smiled, and then said to Patty, "I know this woman. I was driving her all over town three or four days ago."

The woman looked up at me and shook her head. There was no sign of recognition on her face. I know how confusing it can be to unexpectedly meet someone in a completely different setting. It takes the brain a moment to adjust to the new surroundings. I was very happy to see the woman because I'd been concerned about her.

"You probably don't recognize me, but I'm the man who gave you a ride to your sister's house a couple of days ago," I said.

Once again, she shook her head and said no. I knew she had trouble with her memory, so I added a few details, hoping to jog it.

"Don't you remember? You were trying to walk over to your sister's house, but it was too far, so you stopped and rested on a big rock in the lawn, right across the street from my house."

And still, she shook her head. I could see from the look in her eyes that she had no idea who I was.

"You live on Farell Drive, don't you?" I said.

This time it was Patty who responded. She laughed and said, "Oh, wow! This is amazing. Yes, she does."

I smiled at the woman and said, "Your sister lives on Westfield Avenue in Ansonia, off of Wakelee, doesn't she? I drove you over there, but you decided not to ring the doorbell."

By then, I realized that the woman had no memory of what had happened. She just sat there looking confused and uneasy. I certainly wasn't trying to upset her, and I was afraid that if I asked her any more questions, I would.

"Well, I've got a few more errands to run, so I'd better be on my way," I said. "Good to see you, Patty!"

When I reached the door, I turned to wave good-bye. The woman was sitting in the same position she'd been in when I came, clutching the handle of her cane in one hand. I just hoped that someone was going to stop by to pick her up. There was no way that she could have walked from her house to the barber shop. Maybe it was a blessing that she had no memory of what happened three or four days ago. It would only have upset her. She was a sweet woman, overwhelmed by the most ordinary events.

Walking down the street, I said a prayer for the woman and thanked the Lord for showing me that she was all right. It calmed my heart. I should have known. The Lord looks after his lost sheep.

SPEECHLESS

"*I couldn't believe what happened. I was speechless!*"
We've all had that experience. Fortunately, for most of us, it is only temporary. Like our ability to see and hear, we take being able to speak for granted. The loss of vision isolates us from the beauty of the world around us, and the loss of hearing takes away the joy of music and laughter. When we lose our ability to speak, it hits at the heart of our humanity. We lose our ability to talk with others.

Our friends Art and Merle lived across the street from us. Art was very friendly and talkative. He was always willing to help. When we were working out in the yard, one of us would always stop what he was doing and walk across the street for a friendly conversation.

"How you doin', Art?"

"Pretty good," he'd answer. He'd rarely complain.

The first sign that he had Alzheimer's disease was his difficulty in bringing words to mind. I didn't notice it for a long time, but Art knew something was wrong. When he was talking, he'd reach back into his mind for a word, and it wouldn't be there. He'd have to search around and find another word that would work. I didn't notice his pause or the slight awkwardness of the sentence, but

Art was very disturbed about it. As time went by, it became more noticeable to me, and Art became more withdrawn. He was no longer comfortable in conversation. Alzheimer's had robbed me of a friend and neighbor. It wasn't the first time.

Years ago, I played and sang gospel music at a health care center in Stamford, Connecticut, where I was living at the time. You can always spot the residents who used to sing in their church choir. They love to sing along, especially those who once sang leads. In this particular health care center there was a lovely elderly woman who always came to my programs. Even though she was frail, she could still walk, and she'd always take a seat in the row directly in front of me. We'd talk for a bit before I started singing, and she told me that she'd sung leads in her church choir for many years. I found that easy to believe, because she had a lovely voice. I'd sing the old hymns and she knew all the words, and we'd sing them together. Sometimes she'd sing harmony with me, and we had a wonderful time.

And then, suddenly, she stopped coming. I asked the nurses about her and they told me she'd had a stroke. A couple of months later when I came back to do a program, there she was—sitting in a wheelchair, in her usual spot directly in front of me. She gave me a big smile, and I grinned broadly in response. I was so happy to see her! When I went over to talk with her, she tried to respond, but only garbled sounds came out of her mouth. She could no longer speak intelligibly.

I took her hand and told her, "That's all right," and she smiled and seemed relieved that I understood. Grabbing my guitar, I played a few notes and then started singing "What a Friend We Have in Jesus," and she joined me in her sweet, clear voice. I knew she knew the words by heart because she'd sung along with me so many times before, but she couldn't sing them anymore. She just sang along with a broad smile on her face. It was nice to have her back. I couldn't understand a word she sang, but I knew Jesus could, and he must have been very pleased to hear her voice praising him once more. I know I was.

Several years later, I met a wonderful woman at Union Baptist Church in Stamford. I had just joined the church and didn't know anyone, but she came over and sat with me at coffee hour. Mary had been a schoolteacher for many years, and she carried herself with a gentle grace. We had a wonderful conversation, just getting to know each other. She confided in me that she'd had a serious stroke a couple of years earlier, and it left her unable to say a single word. It must have been a blow to someone who spoke so fluently.

"It was a terrible shock to me not to be able to speak," she said.

But Mary wasn't disheartened. She went to the Lord and asked him if it was his will to give her back her speech. She didn't ask for a miracle. She was willing to work. Her first desire was to be able to pray the Lord's Prayer, and that's where she started.

"It took me a long time," she said. "I had to learn to speak the prayer a word at a time, but the Lord was with me, and I finally was able to speak the whole Lord's prayer."

In her desire to praise the Lord in prayer, she fully regained her speech. Sitting there at the table, listening to her story, I marveled at how clearly and feelingly she spoke. The Lord had made a way out of no way.

When we go to the Lord in prayer, there are times when we search for the right words to express our feelings, and to our dismay we are speechless. Sometimes, just being in the presence of the Lord can do that. The apostle Paul offers encouragement to us when the words won't come. God knows our infirmities and sends us the Holy Spirit to speak on our behalf.

> Likewise the Spirit also helpeth our infirmities: for we know not what we should pray for as we ought: but the Spirit itself maketh intercession for us with groanings which cannot be uttered.
> (Romans 8:26)

Not being able to speak intelligibly doesn't always stop someone from talking. George is a resident at a health care center where my wife and I participate in a Tuesday morning church service with our friend Reverend Ken Smith. George can talk anyone under the table. His face lights up, and he gestures with his hands in an animated way. He doesn't seem to be bothered by his inability to say an intelligible word. George played drums in a small band for many years at a nightclub in a hotel in neighboring Ansonia. Or at least that's what he used to tell people when he could still talk. The hotel had long since burned down, and there are probably very few people still living who would remember him or the nightclub. When I am playing and singing, he sways with the music with a big grin on his face, moving his arms in rhythm with the song.

The last time I remember him speaking clearly to me was a year or so ago. I stopped over to see him after the service, as he is always gesturing to me to come. When I came over to his wheelchair that day, he looked up at me enthusiastically and said, "I like your belt. Give it to me."

I was taken aback by how clearly he spoke. "I can't do that, John. My pants would fall down."

He looked up and laughed at me. That seemed to satisfy him.

These days, George is content to sit and listen, speaking enthusiastically with words only God can understand. When I start playing my guitar, he plays along with his hands, beaming broadly. He's the only person I've ever known who plays air guitar duets with me.

Even in our darkest hour, God never forsakes us. Whatever our infirmities, God can put our hearts at rest. We can take comfort in Christ's promise to us.

> Peace I leave with you, my peace I give unto you. Let not your heart be troubled, neither let it be afraid.
>
> (John 14:27)

God knows our every need. All we need to do is speak with our hearts.

PROUD POPPAS

There's nothing like the pride a father feels about his son, just as there is nothing like a mother's love. They say, "He's like a chip off the old block!" The apostle Paul wrote to the men of Gallatia: "And because ye are sons, God hath sent forth the Spirit of his son into your hearts" (Galatians 4:6).

In all the references to God in the Bible, one of the most moving is when Christ was in the garden of Gethsemane contemplating his coming crucifixion on the cross. Jesus turned to his father, not as the creator of the universe, but as his daddy, calling out to him in his distress.

> And he said, Abba, Father, all things are possible unto thee; take away this cup from me; nevertheless, not what I will, but what thou wilt.
> (Mark 14:36)

The word Abba *reflects the personal, intimate relationship Jesus had with his father. It translates closest to our word* daddy. *As earthly daddies, we can understand the love and pride that God has for his children. We feel the same way.*

Few things fill a father's heart with pride as much as when he sees his children treating others lovingly. His chest bursts with pride, and he says to himself, "That's my son!" This was one of those occasions.

On the surface, there was nothing unusual about having dinner at my parents' home with my two sons. For most families, it's a commonplace experience. For us, it was a long-awaited chance for our family to be together. Living a thousand miles away, this was the first time I'd been able to bring my sons home.

Earlier that day, I had taken my sons Gideon and Aaron out shopping, and Aaron had asked if I'd buy him a can of Hubba Bubba soda. From the start, it sounded like a bad idea. At the time, Hubba Bubba was the most popular brand of bubblegum, but the thought of pink, artificially-sweetened, carbonated, bubble-gum-flavored soda was enough to kill my appetite. But we were on vacation, and what's a vacation for if you don't try things that you don't do every day back home?

When we sat down for dinner, the chilled can of Hubba Bubba soda was placed next to Aaron's dish, and as soon as grace was said, he popped the can and took a swig of the soda. I could see from the expression on his face that my suspicions about the wisdom of bubblegum-flavored soda were right. It was all that Aaron could do not to spit it out. The soda went down his throat kicking and screaming.

"Yuck! This stuff is TERRIBLE!" Aaron exclaimed, setting the can down emphatically on the table. "There's no way I'm going drink any more of this!"

"You should always finish anything that is served to you at the table," my father said.

My father took pride in being willing to eat anything, and I know he was raised not to waste food. So was I. The reality was that, while my father might be willing to eat anything, he didn't like 90 percent of everyday dishes, and he'd let you know about it. He liked meat and potatoes with a side dish of vegetables from our garden.

Without missing a step, Aaron asked, "Why don't you taste it, Grandpa?" And the gauntlet was flung. When my father reached over to take the can of Hubba Bubba, the table went silent. All eyes were on him as he lifted the can to his lips and took a sip of the soda. It took all my father's willpower to swallow a mouthful of the soda, and the face he made betrayed his attempt to make it look like he was enjoying the drink. Without saying a word, he sat the can on the table. After a moment's pause, Aaron asked the question that we all wanted to ask.

"How do you like it, Grandpa?" There was no hint of disrespect or sarcasm in Aaron's voice.

"It's good," said my father without much enthusiasm.

And we continued with our meal.

After dinner, with the can sitting untouched on the table, I asked the boys to clear the table and help with the dishes. The can of Hubba Bubba soda was unceremoniously dumped down the kitchen sink without a word from anyone. It was still almost full, with only two sips gone, but no one suggested putting it in the refrigerator. We loved my father too much to do that. The thing that really pleased me was the respectful restraint my sons showed. They could have made it difficult for my father by saying, "Come on, Grandpa! You started drinking that soda, and you said that when you started something at the table, you should finish it." I was a very proud poppa at that moment. They allowed my father to save face without challenging him. When I was their age, I wouldn't have been so gracious.

If I was so proud of my sons, can you imagine how proud God is? With a son as good as Jesus, who wouldn't be? When Jesus took Peter, James, and John up onto the mountain, God spoke out of a cloud and said, "This is my beloved son, in whom I am well pleased" (Matthew 17:5).

Like God, I was well pleased with my sons. And like God, I could say, "These are my beloved sons."

Two proud poppas.

A POMEGRANATE IN A PEAR TREE

Somebody just discovered pomegranates. In America, they are the latest health food fad. Never mind that they've been around for thousands of years. When Moses was called to make a tabernacle to house the ark of the covenant, God's directions were very explicit. He even directed Moses in the creation of the sacred vestments.

> *And beneath upon the hem of it thou shalt make pomegranates of blue and of purple, and of scarlet, round about the hem thereof; and bells of gold between them round about.*
>
> (Exodus 28:33)

Many years later, when Solomon built the temple, pomegranates were prominently displayed on the top of two hundred pillars.

> *And he made the pillars, and two rows round about upon the one network, to cover the chapiters that were upon the top, with pomegranates: and so did he for the other chapter . . . . And the chapiters on the two pillars had pomegranates also above, over against the belly which was by the network: and the pomegranates were two hundred in rows, round about the other chapiter.*
>
> (1 Kings 7:18, 20)

Hopefully, these instructions made more sense to the artisans of Solomon's day than they do to us. A chapiter, by the way, is the *upper part of a column or pillar. It would more likely be called a capital today.*

The lowly pomegranate even had a sensual association. In the Song of Solomon, a woman's temples were compared to pomegranates: "Thy lips are like a thread of scarlet, and thy speech is comely: thy temples are like a piece of pomegranate within thy locks" (Song of Solomon 4:3).

Why were pomegranates so revered in ancient times? The rind and fruit of the pomegranate was used as a remedy against a whole variety of ailments, including diarrhea, dysentery, and intestinal parasites. Pomegranates are a good source of vitamins C and B5 and may be effective in reducing the risk of heart disease by lowering LDL cholesterol levels. The juice of the pomegranate was used as eyedrops. These days there is hardly a fruit juice that isn't sold in a mix with pomegranate juice. Somewhere along the line, the prominence of pomegranates in worship has been lost.

The days were dwindling down to a precious few. Christmas was right around the corner. I was out shopping, picking up a few items as we prepared for the holidays. The lines were long at BJ's Wholesale Club, and I was faced with my usual dilemma: I had to choose which line to get into. It seemed like I always ended up picking the slowest one. As I stood there, slowly inching my way toward the checkout, I noticed the man standing in the line next to me. He had a full beard and was wearing a cream-colored turban. He was standing there calmly, unfazed by the lines, even though all he had in his basket was a cardboard box with four pomegranates in it. I hadn't noticed the pomegranates when I was picking fruit and vegetables, but then, I wouldn't have bought any if I had. I thought of them primarily as Christmas decorations to be placed on the mantle, if you had one, and left there until they shrived up like a prune—and then were unceremoniously dumped into the garbage pail. I didn't know anyone who'd ever eaten one.

The line next to me wasn't moving any faster than the one I was in, so I walked over to the man, rested my arm gently on his shoulder, and said, "Over the years I've seen people use pomegranates for Christmas decorations, but I've never tasted one. How do you eat them? Do you cook them, or eat them like an orange?"

The man turned to me and smiled and said, "No, you cut through the outer skin just enough so that you can peel them open, and then you eat the seeds."

"Just the seeds?" I asked.

"Yes, just the seeds," he said. "Someone told me that the pomegranates in this store are very good this year. Why don't you take one?"

"Oh, I couldn't do that," I said, "You only have four."

"That's all right. Go ahead and take one."

He seemed so genuinely sincere that I relented and said, "Thank you, I'll try one," and I added, "Have a Merry Christmas! Or praise Allah! Whatever your faith is."

He smiled and said, "Thank you." By then we'd both reached the self check-out machines and began checking out our few items.

"They're going to give me a hard time when I try to leave here," I said. "I don't have a receipt for this pomegranate. They'll think I've stolen it."

Just then, one of the clerks came walking by and noticed that my friend was missing a pomegranate. "Where is your other pomegranate?" she asked.

"I gave it to him," he answered, pointing over to me.

The checkout clerk seemed satisfied with his explanation after I held up my lonely pomegranate. She went over to the main counter and picked up the phone to call the woman at the door that checks to make sure no one is trying to get out without a receipt to prove they bought every item.

"There's a man coming out who only has three pomegranates," she said. "Let him through. There'll be another man coming in a couple of minutes and he has the fourth pomegranate. He doesn't need a receipt. It was a gift from the first man."

When I got to the door I recognized the woman checking people's carts. I'd seen her many times before. "I have the missing pomegranate," I said, laughing, and she let me through.

As I was leaving, I called back to her over my shoulder with a twinkle in my eye, just like Santa Claus. "Have a merry Christmas."

The whole experience made me realize how Americanized Christmas has become. You'd think Jesus was born in Cleveland, Santa Claus drinks Coca Cola, and if you don't get your kid an Elmo doll, the holidays will be ruined. It took someone who grew up in the Middle East to remind me that there are treasured customs that predate America by thousands of years. Many of our customs in America come from England and would be as foreign to someone living in Jerusalem in Christ's times as Coca Cola. What in the world is a figgy pudding, and why won't people go home until they get some?

Maybe we should be singing, "And a pomegranate in a pear tree." It would be much more biblical.

HAVE SMILE, WILL TRAVEL

When it comes to the children of God, we are all gifted. We may grow up believing that when it came to handing out talents we got in the wrong line, but that's because we don't recognize our gifts. How many times have you heard someone say, "I wish I had his talent!" They're usually talking about an actor or musician. If you tell them, "We all have talents," they immediately respond, "Not me; I don't have any." Their definition of talent is too limited. I've always loved the passage in Romans where the apostle Paul writes about the body of Christ:

> For as we have many members in one body, all members have not the same office; So we, being many, are one body in Christ, and every one members one of another. Having then gifts differing according to the grace that is given to us, whether prophecy according to the proportion of faith; or ministry, let us wait on our ministering, or he that teacheth on teaching.
>
> (Romans 12:4–7)

And because we are of one body, Paul encourages us:

> Be kindly affectioned one to another with brotherly love; in honor preferring one another. Rejoicing in hope; patient in tribulation; continuing instant in prayer.
>
> (Romans 12:10, 12)

We all have many gifts that the Lord has bestowed on us. Some can sing with the voice of an angel, while others can make an old engine purr like a kitten. Some have a way with words, while others always seem to know exactly what needs to be done when there's a problem. Some gifts may seem grandiose, while others seem too modest to even be thought of as gifts. Any gift used in the service of the Lord is of great value. Something as simple as a smile may be a great blessing to others.

We had just boarded the cruise ship in Amsterdam, our hearts filled with anticipation about visiting Scandinavia and northern Europe. We'd been weeks in preparing, and after a two-hour delay, we finally were cleared to board the ship. Because the cabins weren't ready, we decided to spend some time exploring the ship. With eleven decks, we wouldn't run out of interesting places to see. We'd had a long day waiting to board the ship, and we ran out of energy long before we ran out of ship. After a wrong turn here and there, we ended up in the Seaside Café, more than ready to enjoy a relaxing dinner. With two thousand passengers on board and long lines for the buffet, we were fortunate to find an open table.

No sooner had we sat down and settled in when a woman approached our table. I'd noticed her wandering around looking without success for a place to eat, and there were two unoccupied chairs at our table.

"Do you mind if I join you?" she asked.

"Not at all, please do," I responded.

When I looked up to see her approaching our table, the first thing that struck me was the warmth of her smile. It was the kind of smile you'd expect when you looked up to see an old friend, and yet we'd never met.

"My name is Rita," she said.

"I'm Jerry, and this is my wife, Ruth."

"I'm traveling alone," she said. "My travel agent paired me with a woman who was a single passenger too. We share a cabin, but I really don't know her."

I wasn't surprised to hear that. We'd only been on the ship a couple of hours. But then, it certainly didn't take long for Rita to get to know me and my wife. Her smile was a table-warmer. When someone is at ease with themselves, they put everyone else at ease, and it wasn't long before we were lost in conversation. As it turned out, Rita had lived in Connecticut, not far from where we live, and had moved to Arizona three years ago. She had friends in the town next to ours, and she visited there often. We might easily have passed on the street. Instead, we met in Amsterdam.

In the days that followed, I'd occasionally see Rita. She was usually sitting at a table with people I'd never seen her with before. There is a lot you can tell about a conversation, just with a quick glance. It's not necessary to hear what people are talking about, or even the tone of their voices. I could see Rita and her newfound friends leaning toward each other over the table, listening with rapt attention. One smile begets another, and you could hear the sound of laughter floating across the room.

The only other time we spent with Rita was in St. Petersburg, Russia, where we shared the same tour bus. There wasn't much conversation because our whole group was constantly moving. We did cross paths long enough to take pictures of each other, and we said that we'd keep in touch after the tour.

On the final day of our cruise as we were on our way to dinner, we passed through the Rendezvous Lounge . We'd sat there several times before, listening to the young woman singing old standards with a small three-piece jazz combo called Kathleen and the Saints. The song she was singing as we entered the room was an old familiar one.

> *Light up your face with gladness*
> *Hide every trace of sadness*
> *Although a tear may be ever so near*
> *That's the time you must keep on trying*
> *Smile, what's the use of crying?*
> *You'll find that life is still worthwhile*
> *If you just smile*[31]

And I did.

One thing about a smile: you can take it anywhere. It is as welcome in a checkout counter at the neighborhood supermarket as it is on a cruise ship anchored in the Amsterdam harbor. Smiles can speak volumes. They can offer encouragement and lift the spirits in a way that words sometimes can't.

For the last five years, Ruth and I have participated in a monthly church service at a local health care center with our friend Rev. Ken Smith. Each of us brings a gift. Ken brings the Word and an uplifting message, I bring my guitar and sing three or four gospel songs, and Ruth brings her smile. I'm sure that, for some of the people, her smile does as much to uplift them as the message and the music. Ruth and I usually arrive first, and while I am setting up my guitar and amplifier, Ruth moves around the room, stopping to talk with each of the residents. Many of them recognize Ruth, and I know they look forward to seeing her. She approaches them with an outstretched hand, which she often rests gently on their shoulder.

"How are you doing today?" she asks.

Her smile is reassuring and their faces light up. She reaches down and takes their hand, and for a moment the cares of the day are washed away. They speak openly of their fears and loneliness because they know they can confide in her. The conversations are brief because there are many residents to stop and talk with, but her smile says it all. It says, "I care about you," and when they pour out their heart to her, it says, "You'll be all right; the Lord is with you. He hasn't forgotten you." Smiles speak eloquently.

In the 'fifties, Richard Boone played a gunfighter named Paladin on a TV series. His business card said "Have gun, will travel." You could say the same thing about a smile. Don't leave home without one.

LIFE IN THE SLOW LANE

When you're careening down the road of life, you miss all the side roads that lead to God's blessings. By the time you realize that you've missed a turn, it's disappeared behind you in the rearview mirror and there's no way to turn back.

> *Stop for a minute, enjoy your day*
> *Don't let this moment go slipping away*
> *What's all the hurry, what are you running for?*
> *When you could be taking it easy, with Mister*
> *Sunshine at your door*
>
> *Stop what you're doing, and put it away*
> *Leave a note on the door that you'll be gone for the day*
> *Life's there for living, no need to ask yourself why*
> *'Cause while you're sitting there wondering,*
> *all the good times will pass you by*[32]

Sometimes I think it's not the wrong turns in life that do us in; it's the turns we missed because we were running ahead of God.

Jesus, in his love for us, told us to consider the lilies of the field.

> And why take ye thought for raiment? Consider the lilies of the field, how they grow; they toil not, neither do they spin. And yet I

say unto you, that even Solomon in all his glory was not arrayed like one of these.

(Matthew 6:28–29)

It's hard to see the lilies of the field, let alone consider them when you're driving seventy-five miles an hour in the passing lane. Take your time and slow life down. You'll be surprised at what you will discover.

This is a true story.

When I got my first car in the good old days, it was a 1951 Chevrolet.[33]

Shortly after I got my '51 Chevrolet, a couple of my nephews came up to my parents' house and were admiring my car. Even though it was nine years old, it was still in good shape, and the forest-green paint glistened in the afternoon sun. My nephews asked if I'd take them for a ride, so I loaded them in the car.

"Let's see how fast it can go, Unca Jerry!" they chirped.

"Nah, that's no fun . . . let's see how slow it can go," I answered.

We were driving down the street at two or three miles an hour when a dog spotted us. He raced toward the car, barking ferociously.

Finally, I'll be able to catch a car, he thought.

It only took him a moment to get over to the car, and he naturally shifted into racing gear, expecting to run alongside the car barking wildly until his lungs were bursting. At three miles an hour, though, he would have disappeared out of sight in front of us, so he had to downshift in order to stay next to the car. At first he ran slowly, but he was still running in front of us. It looked like we were chasing him. Finally, he had to walk leisurely alongside my car. By then, my nephews were laughing hysterically at the sight of this confused dog walking next to our car, barking halfheartedly.

"Man, if anyone sees me walking by the side of this car, barking so loudly, my reputation will be ruined," he said to himself. "I'd better get out of here before someone sees me," and he sidled away from the car as unobtrusively as he could, whistling under his breath.

"Me chasing that car? Nah, I was just walking along and this stupid guy and a carload of kids happened to be driving by real slowly." A dog has his pride.

And you know what the Bible has to say about pride: "Pride goeth before destruction, and a haughty spirit before a fall" (Proverbs 16:18).

As I slowly drove away, I could see the dog sitting on his haunches, still looking embarrassed.

If we want to receive all the blessings God has prepared for us, we need to slow down once in a while. We don't ever want to get ahead of God.

MAN KIND

I've always loved words. I think most kids do. They like to make up songs. It seems to come naturally. When my nephews Dan and Tim Bonk were kids, they took the Davey Crockett song from the old television program and gave it a brand new spin.

> *Borned on a mountaintop in Tennessee*
> *Tore his pants on a Christmas tree*
> *Patched them up with some bubble gum*
> *Along came a bear and he asked for some*
>
> *Chorus:*
>
> *Davey, Davey Crockett, king of the wild frontier*
> *Slept on a tabletop in Joe's Café*
> *The greasiest joint in the USA*
> *Ordered a griddley and that ain't all*
> *The next thing I knew I was in City Hall*

When I asked them what a "griddley" was, they said they didn't know. They just liked the sound of the word. I've never lost that appreciation for the playfulness of words, so I added another verse in the same spirit just to finish the song.

*I went to see the mayor just to set him straight
I found him swinging on the pearly gates
He charged me two dollars and he let me go
So I went on down to Mexico*

Words are at the heart of prayer. They're what we use when we talk to God. Sometimes we become tongue-tied, but that's no matter. The Holy Spirit can express the inexpressible for us. Our knowledge of God and Jesus Christ comes to us through words. We even refer to the Bible as the Word. Words can become as familiar as an old armchair. We sink down into them without much thought. They're just there. We've heard them so many times that they've lost their meaning. Sometimes we need someone else to give us a new perspective. This was one of those times.

I was sitting in the barber's chair getting my semiannual haircut when she walked through the front door. She stood there a moment, silhouetted by the brilliant light that flooded the front of the store. Not that I would have recognized her, because I'd never seen the woman before.

"Hey," she called out in a friendly voice. "How you doing, Patty?"

My barber answered back, "Pretty good, how about you?"

"I was just getting bored. I needed a break."

And the conversation was off and running. Although we were never introduced, I figured out from their conversation she must be Michelle, the woman who ran the sewing shop next door. I wandered naturally into the conversation, and we talked about blue jeans and other weighty issues. It was a short conversation, which ended as abruptly as it started.

"Well, I guess I'd better get back to work," she said, and disappeared into the brilliant early spring sunlight as suddenly as she had appeared five minutes earlier.

A couple of days later, I was out shopping in the area and decided that I'd drop off a flyer at Michelle's store. I was going to be doing a "Meet the Author" program at the library in a neighboring town, and although I couldn't remember if she had spoken specifically about her faith, it had shone through in her conversation. When I walked through the door, she recognized me before I had a chance to introduce myself. I showed her the flyer, and we were suddenly deep in a conversation about our faith.

"I go to churches," she said, "and I hear the preacher talking about all the things we shouldn't do. We're supposed to love mankind!" Her voice was ringing with conviction.

"Look at the word *mankind*," she said, pausing between the words *man* and *kind*." We're supposed to be kind to man! If we were kind to each other, that would take care of all the other stuff."

I couldn't agree more.

In the next few days, that conversation kept running through my head. I looked at the word *mankind* in a completely new way. I took it apart. When we use the word *mankind*, we're not talking about male or female. "Man" means the human race. The word *kind* has several meanings. In country music they sing about the cheatin' kind, and we all know what they're talking about. The definition in Merriam-Webster's Dictionary that applies is "a group united by common traits or interests." Wouldn't it be wonderful if, when we look at other people, we could see all that we have in common? If we could remember that we are all God's children, whatever our race, nationality, or beliefs, we'd be well on our way to beginning to understand each other. More often we look for the differences that separate us.

The definition of *kind* that Michelle was talking about is "of a sympathetic or helpful nature." Put together all three of those definitions of the two words and you start to see that we are all united because we are children of God, and we are to treat each other with kindness and sympathy. Christ stated it much more eloquently.

> Thou shalt love the Lord thy God with all thy heart and with all thy soul, and with all thy mind. This is the first and great commandment. And the second is like unto it, Thou shalt love thy neighbor as thyself. On these two commandments hang all the law and the prophets.
>
> (Matthew 22:37–40)

Loving your neighbor as yourself is a challenge that most of us aren't up to. Charles Schultz, creator of the *Peanuts* cartoon strip, put his finger on the problem as he so often did. In one of his strips, he captured a conversation between Lucy and Linus. In the first frame, Lucy is skipping rope and calls to Linus, "You, a doctor? HA, that's a big laugh!" In the next frame she walks over to Linus and faces him, almost nose to nose. "You could never be a doctor, you know why?" As she resumes jumping rope, she calls back over her shoulder, "Because you don't love mankind, that's why!" In the last frame, Linus is calling to her, "I love mankind . . . it's PEOPLE I can't stand!!" Schultz was a wise man. Loving mankind in theory is one thing, but trying to love someone when they are treating you badly often takes more goodness than we can muster.

Christ often spoke in absolutes. He didn't leave much wiggle room. "Be ye therefore perfect, even as your Father, which is in heaven is perfect" (Matthew 5:48).

How can we possibly live up to all the commandments Jesus gave us? Consider the alternative. What if Christ had said, "Love your neighbors—except Bill, who borrowed your electric drill and never returned it?" Once you start making exceptions, you lose the power of the commandment. It becomes more of an advisement. If he said, "Be ye pretty good, but I realize that you can't be anywhere near as good as your Father in heaven," what kind of a commandment would that be? There would be too many loopholes. We could all hop on for a free ride. There are no free rides when it comes to serving the Lord. Instead, we strive for perfection, knowing full well that we can never achieve it, just as we try our best to love mankind, even though, like Linus, there are people we just can't stand.

Just be thankful Jesus didn't say, "Like your neighbor as you like yourself." For starters, people who deep down don't like themselves probably wouldn't like their neighbors either. It's better to set the bar at perfection and then try to reach it, no matter how far short of the glory we fall. Being kind to man is a good starting point, but we are called to something much higher. And who would have thought that the second commandment was hidden in that armchair-comfortable old word *mankind*. In breaking it into two words, Michelle had found a deeper meaning in a commonplace word.

On Sunday when my wife and I went to Union Baptist in Stamford, we had a guest preacher, Reverend Anderson Clary, Jr. from Hampton, Virginia. His sermon was like a continuation of that brief conversation in Michelle's store. He spoke about compassion as a defining quality of a true Christian: kindness taken to a higher level. Christianity is much more than a book of rules. God judges our works by our hearts. Many a good work is done for selfish reasons. In talking about the Pharisees, Christ spoke of the shallowness of their works: "But all their works they do to be seen of men" (Matthew 23:5).

Good works flow naturally out of a compassionate heart.

The Bible is filled with descriptions of Christ's compassion. When Jesus and his disciples were departing from Jerusalem, a great multitude followed them.

> And behold two blind men sitting by the way side, when they heard that Jesus passed by, cried out, saying, Have mercy on us, O Lord, thou son of David. And the multitude rebuked them, because they should hold their peace; but they cried the more, saying, Have mercy on us, O Lord, thou son of David. And Jesus stood still, and called them, and said, What would ye that I shall do unto you? They say unto him, Lord, that our eyes be opened. So Jesus had compassion on them, and touched their eyes; and immediately their eyes received sight, and they followed him.
> (Matthew 20:29–34)

It was because of his compassion that Christ was moved to feed the multitude of four thousand who were following him.

> Then Jesus called his disciples unto him, and said, I have compassion on the multitude, because they continue with me now for three days, and have nothing to eat.
> (Matthew 15:32)

Perhaps the most moving two words in the Bible tell of Christ's response when he reached the home of his friend Lazarus, who had died. When he asked Martha and Mary where they had laid him, "They said, Lord, come and see. Jesus wept" (John 11:34-35).

The greatest expression of Christ's compassion was when he hung on the cross, in excruciating pain. Even then, Christ felt compassion for those who were crucifying him and prayed to his father, "Forgive them, for they know not what they do" (Luke 23:34).

We are to be obedient to God's will, and it is right that we should fear God. But let us serve him out of love, and with compassion.

The word of God knows no limits. It flows from the pulpit to the barber shops of Main Street. Let us treat each other with kindness and compassion, as God treats us. How can we do less?

"'TWAS THE NIGHT BEFORE CHRISTMAS"

He's a jolly old man with a white beard, red suit, and a potbelly. He has a twinkle in his eye, and he has a habit of placing his finger against the side of his nose when he smiles. When I was a kid, he had a fondness for cookies and cold milk. More recently, he seems to have switched to Coca Cola—if you believe all the ads around Christmas time. He was first known as Saint Nicholas, which was shortened to Saint Nick. Somewhere along the line he became Santa Claus. Maybe that was after he got married. As far as I can figure, he and Mrs. Claus never had children.

Sometimes people seem to confuse God with Santa Claus. He has a white beard, too, if you believe the drawings and paintings. That's a guess, though, because no one has ever seen God. If Santa is old, God is literally older than the hills. After all, he made them.

When Christmas rolls around, the images of God and Santa cross paths. For some people, Christmas comes but once a year, and so does God. That's the time when they go to their annual church service.

There's one other similarity between God and Santa in some people's minds. Santa knows when you are sleeping and when you are awake. So does God. God knows much more, though. He is omniscient. He knows your every weakness. If you are really good (or at least that's what I was told when I was a kid), Santa would give you a lot of cool stuff. God is quite different. God's gifts are far richer, and they aren't a reward for good acts. God's grace is not dependent upon how we live. We can't earn it. He is not making a list and checking it twice, like Santa. God's gifts are much more lasting. They're not like the presents we receive at Christmas that end up broken or discarded in a few months. The greatest gift God has given to us is his son, Jesus Christ. That's why we celebrate Christmas.

The word Christmas *is formed from two words,* Christ *and* mass, *and literally means "Christ celebration." In the hustle and bustle of Christmas, lines blur, and it's easy to get swept up in the spirit of the season, but not in the Spirit.*

When I was a little boy, Santa and Jesus lived comfortably side by side at Christmas. I loved the Christmas story (not the movie, the Bible story.) It was new and exciting, every Christmas. But I was still a kid, and while I believed in Santa until I went to kindergarten, I had my suspicions. I might have been even more suspicious if my father hadn't seen Santa every Christmas. I never saw Santa personally, but my father's description of him was very convincing.

> *When I was a child, I spake as a child, I understood as a child, I thought as a child; but when I became a man, I put away childish things.*
>
> (1 Corinthians 13:11)

When I became a man, I came to know how loving and generous God is. Nobody beats God's giving.

'Twas the night before Christmas, and we'd already opened our presents. Forget the dancing sugar plums. If you ever wondered how Santa Claus could deliver presents to all the kids on earth in one night, it was because he got a running start by bringing all the kids in the Midwest their presents early on Christmas Eve. In our house, Christmas Eve started the minute we finished wolfing down our supper. It was the one time of year when I was thankful that we ate at four o'clock.

Before I was school-age, Santa came to our house every Christmas Eve. He didn't come down the chimney. If he had, he'd end up in our coal furnace, and it wouldn't just be his suit that would be red. He boldly walked through our front door. Not that I'd ever really seen him come into the house. But my Dad had.

After supper, Dad would hide behind the living room davenport, and Mom would herd my sisters and me down onto the basement stairs and then close the door behind us. For some unknown reason, Dad always got to hide behind the davenport so that he could see Santa Claus when he came in.

As soon as the door was closed, Dad would quietly sidle out from behind the davenport and tiptoe across the room and into the bedroom where our presents were carefully hidden in our one closet. He'd quickly carry them into the living room and place them haphazardly under the Christmas tree. When the presents were all under the tree, he would tiptoe across the living room floor and into the dining room and carefully open the front door. With a sigh of relief, he would softly stroll out to the front of the porch and pause for a moment.

Coming back into the house, Dad was Santa Claus. No need for a suit or cotton-ball beard. The only one who could see him was him. As he came striding across the front porch, he'd stomp the nonexistent snow off his nonexistent boots, and when he opened the front door he'd call out a "Ho, ho, ho!" in his best Santa voice. Once inside the house, he'd make a lot of fuss in the living room, as if he were unloading presents from his sack.

All that time, I was hunched breathlessly behind the basement door, visualizing his every move. When the presents were in place, Santa didn't have to stop and eat a plateful of cookies and drink a glass of milk on the way out. We never left anything for him. We didn't want Santa to stick around, once he'd delivered our presents. Besides, he would have preferred a cold Pabst Blue Ribbon, but that would have blown his cover.

As Dad headed noisily out the front door, he'd call over his shoulder, "Ho, ho, ho, and a merry Christmas to all!" and stomp his way across the front porch only to pause there once again. Then, it was a matter of sneaking back into the house without our hearing him so that he could hide behind the davenport. Mom always gave him enough time by telling us that we couldn't come out until we were sure he was gone, or we'd scotch the whole thing.

Mom would cautiously open the door, and we'd all burst into the living room. Or, at least I would burst. I'd be full of excitement, and would start grilling Dad about what he'd seen.

"Did you see him, Dad?"

"Oh, yeah. I peeked around the corner of the davenport when he was putting the presents under the tree," he answered.

"Did you see his reindeer?"

"Naw. I couldn't see them from behind the davenport, but I heard their bells when they took off."

That was enough for me. It never occurred to me to ask the really hard questions like, "If he had all that snow on his boots, how come he didn't track any into the house?" Mom would have had a fit! Or, "How come there aren't any tracks in the snow in our front yard?" By then, the only question I had was "Can we open the presents now?"

When I got older and realized that Santa Claus was my mom and dad, and I had been lovingly duped—not just by Mom and Dad, but by my sisters—Christmas took on more meaning. One thing about Mom, though. She always made it clear that Christmas wasn't just about getting presents. The most important thing was that it was a time to celebrate the birth of the baby Jesus. Those first few years, Santa Claus and the baby Jesus got along real well together, and I loved them both. It wasn't until I was four or five that I realized that only Jesus was real.

THE GRACIOUSNESS OF STRANGERS

*M*any years ago, my wife, Ruth, and I were visiting a man from our church who was on the sick and shut-in list. Neither of us knew him, but that never stopped us from visiting a person. When people are sick, they're happy if anyone comes to visit them. Curtis had been a member of our church for many years long before I joined, and it was only after his passing, when I talked to some of his old friends, that I really felt like I knew him. Earlier in his life he'd been extremely active in the church. His warm personality and sense of humor drew people to him. He was a thin little man, and his friends called him Pee Wee. By the time we first visited him, his wife had long since passed away, and he was living alone in a modest apartment. It must have been a hard change for someone as outgoing and sociable as Curtis to end up sitting in a small apartment day after day, with only an occasional visitor to break the monotony. The few times we visited, he always invited us to sit on the couch and spend some time with him.

Curtis had a number of serious health problems, including diabetes, that had already cost him one leg. The diabetes had taken its toll on his heart too, and he had a pacemaker installed to keep it beating. It was a lonely life. A visiting nurse stopped by once a day, but the rest of the time he was limited to his wheelchair. On one of our visits, the conversation wandered on to football. I expected he would *be a New York Giants fan because we were living close to New York City. That wasn't the case. He loved the Green Bay Packers. It tickled him that a city of less than 100,000 could produce a professional team that had dominated the National Football League for so many years. When I told him my wife and I were going out to visit our family in Wisconsin, his eyes lit up.*

"Will you bring back a Green Bay Packers cap for me?" he asked.

"You can count on it, Curtis!" I answered.

"When will you be back?" he asked.

"In a couple of weeks," I replied. I knew he'd be counting the days.

After we returned from Wisconsin, one of the first things we wanted to do was to bring Curtis his Green Bay Packers cap. We didn't want to keep him waiting.

When we arrived at Curtis's apartment, we rang the doorbell, and a woman we'd never seen before answered the door.

"We've come to visit Curtis," I said, and I heard a faint voice calling from the other room.

"He's had a bad fall," she said. "He just got home from the hospital."

"What happened?" I asked.

"He fell out of his bed and couldn't get back up. He was lying on the floor until I came to visit the next day."

When Ruth and I walked into the bedroom, he was lying on his side with his back facing us.

"Did you remember to bring me my Green Bay Packers cap?" he asked weakly, unable to turn his head to look at us.

"You know I wouldn't forget you, Curtis," I answered. I walked around the side of his bed and leaned over. Gently lifting his head off the pillow, I slid the Green Bay Packers cap onto his head and softly laid his head back on the pillow.

"You're looking good, Curtis!" I said, and a broad grin spread across his drawn face.

"You didn't forget!" he said.

I think not forgetting was even more important than the cap. A couple of weeks later he was gone. I suspect he wore his Green Bay Packers cap when he walked up to St. Peter on two strong legs.

The Graciousness of Strangers

Looking back on that time, I can't help but think about the Good Samaritan. When we see someone in need, it makes no difference if we know them. Anyone in need is our neighbor. Christ, in talking with a young lawyer who was trying to trap him, told the story of a man who was left nearly dead along the side of the road.

> *But he, willing to justify himself, said unto Jesus, and who is my neighbor? And Jesus answering said, A certain man went down from Jerusalem to Jericho, and he fell among thieves, which stripped him of his raiment, and wounded him, and departed, leaving him half dead. And by chance there came down a certain priest that way, and when he saw him, he passed by on the other side. And likewise, a Levite, when he was at the place, came and looked on him, and passed by on the other side. But a certain Samaritan, as he journeyed, came where he was; and when he saw him, he had compassion on him . . . . Which one of these three thinkest thou, was neighbor unto him that fell among the thieves?*
>
> (Luke 10:29–33, 36)

You never know when God will place a person in your path who needs help. They may be a complete stranger. The Good Samaritan didn't ask questions of the man lying on the side of the road. It wasn't important what the man's race or nationality was, or who he voted for in the last election. The Samaritan saw a neighbor in need. That was enough.

It must have been the Green Bay Packers cap that did it. As soon as I walked through the door of Kentucky Fried Chicken, Frank, the manager asked, "You a Green Bay Packers fan? They're going to have a real good team this year. What'd you think about Favre signing with the Vikings?"

It wasn't that I was such a big Packers fan. It was just that when I'd go home to Wisconsin to visit my family, I'd get swept up in the rivalry between the Packers and the Chicago Bears. I remember one Christmas Day when almost everyone showed up late for our family gathering because the Packers game was on. One summer when I was in the local Walmart, I saw a Packers cap at a good price and couldn't resist buying it. I never knew I would be such a hit at a KFC a thousand miles away.

Over the next few months, I started to get to know some of the people who worked there. Justin was particularly friendly. He got a big kick out of my ordering three or four sweet potato pies, and when he'd see me walking through the door, he'd smile and raise his hand with three or four fingers held up.

"How many pies you want, big guy?" I had become "big guy."

The women behind the counter were friendly too, and we'd engage in lively conversation while I was waiting for my order. But Justin was the "Man." After a while, he started giving me his employee discount when he waited on me. Or, if he saw me come in when he was working on the drive-up window, he'd slide over to whoever was waiting on me and quietly say, "Give him my discount." Then Matt got into the act.

"How you doing, cowboy?" Matt would call out when he saw me coming in. I have no idea where he got the cowboy image. It made me smile every time he'd greet me. I remember back in the 'sixties when I was living in New York City, I saw a photo in the newspaper of John F. Kennedy with the caption, "President Kennedy visits the West." The picture was taken in Pennsylvania. I guess that makes Wisconsin the Far West and me a cowboy. It finally reached a point where I felt like family when I stopped by to pick up some grilled chicken and sweet potato pies. I couldn't quite figure out how it happened. I was just a stranger when I started going there.

Back in the early 'sixties, I lived in New York City for four years. It's a city of strangers. I remember seeing a man lying on the sidewalk, with people stepping around him as they passed by. One man stopped to let his dog sniff the man, but no one bothered to see if he needed any help. Samaritans are in short order in New York City. The city motto is "don't get involved." I knelt down on the sidewalk next to him to ask if I could help him, and he could barely talk. I noticed he had a thin plastic bracelet like they wear in the hospital, and I was concerned that he'd had a relapse. Standing in a phone booth across the street while I was calling the police,

I could see the steady flow of people sidestepping him like water flowing around a rock. No one stopped to help.

When the police arrived, the first thing they did was stand me up against the side of the police car and frisk me. I suppose that my actions were suspicious—I was a Samaritan. When they were convinced that I wasn't dangerous, they gave their attention to the man lying on the sidewalk. They loaded him into their police car like a piece of luggage and drove off. I hoped they were taking him to a hospital. I knew then that, as soon as I could, I had to get out of the city.

As always, Christ gets right to the heart of the matter. When he told the story of the Good Samaritan to the lawyer and asked him which of the three men who had passed the man lying on the roadside was his neighbor, the passage reads: "And he said, He that showed mercy on him. Then said Jesus unto him, Go, and do thou likewise" (Luke 10:37).

Whether it's a Green Bay Packers cap, an employee discount, or a phone call to get help for a sick man lying on the sidewalk, Christ calls us to show mercy. We never know when we will be dependent on the graciousness of strangers.

ELIZABETH COTTON'S BANJO

*M*usic has always been an integral part of worship. There was a time when musicians were a part of the workforce when temples were built. That makes sense. If sailors sang sea chanteys on whaling ships, and convicts sang work songs while laying railroad tracks, why wouldn't musicians sing songs of praise when a temple was being built? It could help lift the spirit and remind people whom they were working for. When David prepared to build the temple, he called for the hiring of musicians to prophesy.

> Moreover, David and the captains of the host separated to the service of the sons of Asaph, and of Heman, and of Jeduthun, who should prophesy with harps, psalteries, and with cymbals . . . . All these were under the hands of their father for song in the house of the Lord, with cymbals, psalteries, and harps, for the service of the house of God . . . . So the number of them, with their brethren that were instructed in the songs of the Lord, even all that were cunning, was two hundred fourscore and eight.
>
> (1 Chronicles 25:1, 6–7)

Later, when Josiah repaired the temple, he called upon musicians to oversee the work:

And the men did the work faithfully: and the overseers of them were Jahath and Obadiah, the Levites, of the sons of Merari; and Zechariah and Meshullam, of the sons of the Kohathites, to set it forward; and other of the Levites, all that could skill of instruments of music.
(2 Chronicles 34:12)

There are many references to stringed instruments in the Bible. "Praise him with the timbrel and dance: praise him with stringed instruments and organs" (Psalm 150:4). Back in the Bible days there weren't any banjos. If there had been banjos, they certainly would have used them to praise the Lord.

In the 'sixties, when Bob Dylan and Peter, Paul, and Mary were playing for crowds of thousands, and folk music had broken into the top forty, there was a smaller, quieter revival going on that passed almost unnoticed. The old musicians who had shaped the music for most of their lives were being rediscovered. They didn't play large auditoriums or large festivals. Most of them were playing in small clubs with even smaller crowds. One of those musicians was Elizabeth Cotton. Many years ago, Elizabeth was a maid for the Seeger family and taught Pete, Mike, and their sister Peggy how to finger-pick guitar. They in turn passed her songs and guitar style on to countless young pickers, and her song "Freight Train" became standard fare for folk musicians around the world.

When I heard that Elizabeth Cotton was going to be playing at the Pickin' Parlor in New Haven, I jumped at the chance to hear her. The Pickin' Parlor was run by Harry Guffee and his wife, Ruth. Ruth had a doctorate in Russian literature, and she and Harry were both musicians. Harry looked a little bit like Tom Selleck, and he and Ruth both wore cowboy hats.

The Pickin' Parlor was in a run-down building in a run-down neighborhood. Both had seen their better days. When you walked inside and your eyes adjusted to the dim lighting, you could make out a small stage on one side of the room with a few mismatched folding chairs randomly scattered around it. The walls were lined with old instruments, photos, and posters, and an occasional display case.

Elizabeth Cotton's Banjo

When it was time for the concert to start, Harry gave Elizabeth Cotton a warm introduction and reached down to give her a hand up onto the stage. Taking her time, she shuffled across the stage and eased herself down into a small chair. When she greeted the audience and thanked them for coming, it was as if she'd just invited us into her living room. She was in her early nineties then, and was at the end of the line as a performer. She had a very modest, offhanded way of speaking, and there was an intimacy that night because the crowd was small. Certainly, the crowd was no measure of what a national treasure she was.

When Elizabeth was softly introducing her songs, she told a story about when she was a little girl. Her older brother had a banjo, and she couldn't resist trying to play it. She had no idea what to do with the banjo, but she loved to hold it, and she kept tuning the strings up until one of them would break from the tension. She knew she was in trouble when that happened, so she put the banjo back under the bed, where her brother kept it hidden from her. When he came, the first thing he did was check the banjo, and when he found a string was broken, he knew who'd done it. And Elizabeth caught hell. She wasn't explicit about the terms of that hell, but whatever they were, they didn't stop her. When he'd go out the next time, she'd go find the banjo, try to tune it up, and break a string once again. She told the story with a wistfulness in her voice and said softly that she'd always wanted to have a banjo, but never had one.

As we were sitting there, transfixed by the story, Harry got up and walked over to the wall next to the stage. Without hesitation, he reached up and carefully lifted down a banjo that was hanging there. He quietly walked over to Elizabeth and handed her the banjo, saying, "Now you've got a banjo of your own."

I don't remember what the banjo looked like, and I don't remember exactly what Elizabeth said—or Harry either, for that matter. The words aren't important. It is the memory of the love that Harry, his wife, and every one of us felt for Elizabeth that still remains. And I thought of one of the old hymns she sang.

I shall have a crown to wear when I get home
I shall have a crown to wear when I get home
On the road to glory, I shall tell a story
The Lord will be with me when I get home[34]

When she gets home, I know she'll be carrying that banjo.

THE IMPOSSIBLE JUST TAKES LONGER

And Jesus said unto them, verily I say unto you, if ye have faith as a grain of mustard seed, ye shall say unto this mountain, Remove hence to yonder place; and it shall remove; and nothing shall be impossible to you.

(Matthew 17:20)

*B*ack when I was at the University of Wisconsin, I was living in a rooming house with thirteen other guys. By then, I'd been playing guitar for three or four years, and with the exception of three or four lessons, I was self-taught. In the evening, I'd sit in my room, softly playing my Fender electric guitar, and friends would occasionally wander in to listen.

One friend in particular kept telling me how much he wanted to play guitar. "I'd give my right arm to be able to play guitar," he'd say.

I'd look at him and answer, "If you want to learn to play guitar, give me fifteen minutes of your time every day and I can teach you what I know."

"Fifteen minutes?" he'd say, "I don't have the time for that!"

I used to kid him, saying, "You'd give your right arm to learn to play guitar, but not fifteen minutes a day?" If I'd been up on my Bible, I would have told him to "Remove hence to yonder place!"

I believe Jesus when he said, "Nothing shall be impossible to you." But if you want something to happen, you can't just wish on a star. The only similarity between Jiminy Cricket and Jesus Christ is they have the same initials. Wishing doesn't cut it. Sometimes you have to roll up your sleeves and get to work. Faith alone will not get it done. James 2:17 says, "Even so faith, if it hath not works, is dead, being alone."

If you commit yourself to serving the Lord, he will give you all you need to accomplish his work. But don't expect it to be easy.

> *No matter what they tell you there's no free lunch.*
> *No guaranteed money in the bank*
> *You can't get to heaven in an easy chair*
> *You've got to give it everything it takes*[35]

God don't abide no easy-chair Christians.

The swimming pool stood there dark and menacing, like something out of a Stephen King story. In its youth, it was bright and vibrant, and the air was filled with laughter as children splashed gaily in its waters. But time had not been kind to it. The children had long since grown up and moved away, and the once sky-blue lining had turned a murky dark green. Sitting at my computer in my downstairs office, I was haunted by the tales my neighbor George told of the time the pool burst, spilling four feet of water loaded with chemicals onto the neighboring back yards. It had taken a long time for the lawns to recover. The pool was just ten feet from the window well to my office, and I could picture a torrent of water cascading into the room. Never having owned an above-ground swimming pool, I had no idea what the lifespan of a pool liner was, but I was getting nervous about ours. It was time to get some professional advice.

When I walked into the pool supply store, the man greeted me with a friendly hello. I'd certainly given him enough business over the last seven years for him to smile broadly when he saw me come in.

"I want to find out about replacing a pool liner," I said.

"How old is it?" he asked.

"I'm not sure," I said. "What kind of money am I looking at to replace it?"

"How big is the pool?" he asked, and I told him thirty feet in diameter.

"The pool lining, installed, is going to run you about sixteen hundred dollars," he said.

"We haven't used the pool for three years," I responded, "and I don't know how old the pump and filtration system is. That sounds like more money than makes sense to me. How long a lifetime do pool liners have?" I asked nervously.

"Eight to ten years," he answered.

"My liner has got to be pushing ten years at least. We've been in the house seven years, and the liner didn't look anywhere near new when we moved in."

I thanked the man for the information, walked out the door, and drove back home. Standing there in the back yard, glowering at the pool, I remembered that scriptural promise about having faith even as small as a grain of mustard seed, and the song we used to sing with my gospel quartet, The Gospel Messengers, came to my mind. One line says, "All things are possible, if you only believe."[36]

I looked at the pool and said to it, "Remove ye hence," but nothing happened. Maybe faith can move mountains, but it doesn't work on swimming pools. I couldn't see any way around it. It would cost at least a couple thousand dollars to have the pool taken down and have everything hauled away. I was going to have to take the pool down by myself.

The morning finally arrived when I summoned up enough courage to tackle the job. I went out armed with a large screwdriver and a small saber saw. The first task was to remove the top ledge of the pool. I knew I had my work cut out for me. Over the years, the pool had been painted several times, and the slots in the large bolts that held the top on were dim memories. But, with a lot of patience and an aerosol can of WD-40, I finally got enough of the bolts out so I could start cutting up the metal sides. I'd already drained the pool, so I cut out a six-foot section of the wall and started cutting out the pool liner. My worst fears were confirmed when I had drained the water out of the pool. The seam in the liner looked like it was starting to come apart. We had been living on borrowed time.

With the help of my wife, Ruth, I cut the pool liner into strips, which she rolled up so that we could load them into the car. Then I slowly cut up the rest of the wall in six-foot sections, which Ruth folded in half, ready to take to the dump. After many trips to the dump, I was ready to start breaking up the concrete sidewalk around the pool so that I could remove the metal posts that had held up the sides. For that job, I enlisted my son-in-law, Pasha, to help.

The next morning, Pasha and I went down to the local Home Depot and rented a jackhammer. We'd rented one once before to bust up the concrete bases of a couple of fence posts, and I tried my hand at the jackhammer for a couple of minutes just to say I'd done it. I knew this would take a lot more than a couple of minutes.

We started at nine, alternating between operating the jackhammer and loading the busted-up concrete into a wheelbarrow and dumping it near the fence on the edge of our property. Ruth assisted with picking up concrete, and watched to make sure we didn't jackhammer the power cord. If that had happened, we would have gone on to glory on the spot.

When we'd removed the sidewalk, the first thing we discovered was the metal rim that held the base of the wall together was so badly rotted that, in spots, you could crumple it between your fingers. We'd taken the pool down just in time. The most unexpected discovery was a solid ring of concrete eight inches wide. We started to dig it out, and when we got down a foot, we hit a concrete footing. We started to dig out from the concrete rim to see how wide the footing was, but after a width of a foot, we still hadn't found the edge. We stood there scratching our heads, wondering what the wall could possibly have supported, because it was larger than the old pool. Maybe it was an ancient structure built by the Druids: Connecticut Stonehenge. Whatever it was, we knew we'd have to break several inches off the top of the wall if I were ever to have a lawn in the area. Chipping the top off a solid wall was much harder than busting up the sidewalk, but we had no choice. Sometimes you have to do what you have to do. The whole job took five hours, without taking a lunch break.

After working in the blazing sun for many hours, our bodies were really dragging. It was probably hardest on Pasha because he is a Muslim and he was observing Ramadan. Ramadan honors the month in which the first verses of the Qur'an were revealed to the Islamic prophet Muhammad. It is observed by fasting in order to teach patience, modesty, and spirituality. During those thirty days, Muslims are not allowed to eat or drink while the sun is up. Pasha had eaten his breakfast before sunrise that morning, and even though we were working in the hot midday sun, he couldn't drink any water.

As we stood there leaning on the jackhammer and shovel for support, our conversation turned to Islam and our differing faiths. Pasha was raised in the Christian faith but converted to Islam back in the 'sixties. We've had many long respectful conversations about our faiths, seeking common ground rather than arguing about our differences. We both serve the same God, and when I say grace over meals, I always lift our prayers in the name of our Savior Jesus Christ and Allah.

I had just watched a program on television the night before, discussing the difference between Sunnis and Shiites, so I asked Pasha, "Are you a Sunni or a Shiite, or do those terms even apply to Muslims in this country?"

"I'm a Sunni Muslim," Pasha answered.

Sunni Muslims emphasize those passages in the Qur'an that speak of the sanctity of life and believe that suicide is a sin. The Shiites interpret other passages in the Qur'an that they believe justify suicide when done in the service of the Lord. Acts of terrorism are elevated to holy missions, with the perpetrator raised to glory for their acts. Shia Muslims make up less than a third of the Muslim world but are in the majority in Iraq, Iran, and Lebanon. As a Sunni, Pasha believes that encouraging suicide is a distortion of the teachings of the Qur'an. And we were launched into another discussion on religion.

Working there in the relentless sunlight, I thought back to the 'sixties and the young kids who wandered into the coffeehouses in Greenwich Village, lost in the romance of folk songs. They'd get up on stage at the hootenannies and solemnly pronounce that they were going to do an authentic work song from the chain gangs of the South. When they sang, they'd utter a "whumpp" and then let out a grunt, pretending that they were swinging a nine-pound hammer, while plucking the bass string on their guitar with a little more force. Pasha and I weren't singing "Take this hammer and carry it to the captain," and whatever grunts we might have emitted were hard earned. We were exhausted from the heat and the weight of the jackhammer. After working for five hours with a ninety-pound jackhammer that rattled the fillings in your teeth, a nine-pound hammer sounded pretty good.

The morning after our road-gang workout, I expected to awaken aching from head to toe. I'm not used to such heavy physical work. To my surprise, I felt better than I had in months. I guess all that work loosened up my old muscles and stretched me out. It was good it had, because the hard work was still to come. I was faced with getting rid of what looked like a ton of sand, as well as the mountain of busted concrete we had created. I had talked briefly to my buddies Ralph and John down at the city dump about bringing the sand there, but we hadn't gotten down to specifics. In the last few weeks with all the trips I'd taken to the dump, I'd spent more time with the two of them than I had with almost anybody other than my wife.

The next day, when I took another load of the cut-up swimming pool to the dump, I stopped and talked to Ralph.

"Hey, Ralph, I need some help," I said. "I've got a ton of sand to get rid of, and you said that I could bring it here. How does that work?"

"You can bring it here a carload at a time and dump it, or if you're interested, we have a small dumpster you can rent," he answered. "We can deliver it to your house, and when you fill it half full, we'll come and pick it up, and then bring it back for a second load."

"How much does that cost?" I asked.

"Two hundred and fifty bucks," he replied.

"That sounds a little steep for me," I said. "How much does it cost if I bring it here a carload at a time?" I asked.

"Six dollars a ton," he answered.

"Let me think about it. Thanks for the information," I responded.

The next morning I had a heart-to-heart conversation with my contractor. I looked in the mirror and asked him, "So, what do you think I should do? We're a little short of help these days, with the economy being what it is, so you're the only worker. How do you feel about hauling a ton of sand a wheelbarrow at a time until you fill a dumpster?" I figured it was going to be hard enough to haul the sand out of there a carload at a time. I couldn't imagine having to do the whole job by myself in two or three days. Besides, six dollars a ton sounded a lot better than the two-hundred-and-fifty-dollar rental. There was something oddly appealing about the seemingly impossible job of hauling a ton of sand to the dump a few bags at a time.

My next trip to the dump I brought eight bags of sand I'd loaded into the heaviest trash bags they sold at Walmart, and pulled up to the weighing station. Ralph gave me the high sign after he'd written down the weight of my car, and I drove to the edge of the dump and emptied the bags. When I drove back onto the weighing platform, Ralph weighed my car again to see how much sand I'd dumped.

"So, how much is the damage?" I asked.

"You owe me forty-eight cents," he said, and we both laughed.

Two and a half weeks later my tab had risen to six dollars, and I realized I'd hauled a ton of sand. I was just a little over a quarter of the way done. I could see that my ability to estimate what a ton of sand looked like left a lot to be desired. I don't remember ever having seen a ton of sand before. They say that when the prayers go up, the blessings come down. I'd prayed for the strength to do the impossible, and the Lord answered my prayers with several tons of blessings.

It was just going to take longer than I had planned on. And I sang to myself under my breath:

Lord, don't move this sand pile
Just give me the strength to take it to the dump

I ended up taking more than three tons of sand to the dump, eight bags at a time. And finally, the pool moved hence. Praise the Lord!

How do you get rid of three tons of sand? A bag at a time. Sometimes it's best not to pray for a miracle. If you use the resources the Lord has blessed you with, you can get the job done, on God's time.

KHRISTIE, BRIAN, AND ST. LUKE

"*Serendipity: The faculty or phenomenon of finding valuable or agreeable things not sought for.*" (Merriam-Webster's Collegiate Dictionary)

In God there is no serendipity. He knows what he's doing, and he always has a plan. His ways are not our ways, and right smack dab in the middle of an ordinary day, he will bless us with treasures of the heart.

I swung into the parking lot of the Sunoco station and slipped into an open parking space. I reached over on the front seat and grabbed my Bible. I'd been working on a story that morning, and I'd tucked it in the Bible in case inspiration dropped by while I was having the oil changed in my car. I never know when that might happen. When I walked into the office of the station, there was a young woman working behind the counter who I didn't remember seeing before.

"Good morning," I said. "How is your schedule today? Do you have the time to do an oil change?"

"Sure, that won't be any problem," she answered. "We can have your car in here in five or ten minutes. We should have you out of here in a half hour. Do you want to wait?"

I had thought of walking over to the Super Stop and Shop a few blocks away to do some shopping while the car was being worked on, but on second thought, sitting down sounded like a better idea.

"That sounds good," I said. "I have my Bible with me, so I won't run out of things to read."

When I walked over to sit in a chair in the waiting area, I noticed Brian. Not that I knew who he was. That came later. We exchanged a quick hello, and then Khristie come over and leaned on the counter. By then, I'd pulled out the pages of the story I was working on, intending to jot down some ideas.

"I'm working on a book," I said to her. "That should keep me busy."

"I love to read," she said. "I'm never without a book."

"I'm glad to know that someone still reads," I said. "Books seem to be going out of fashion. This will be my second book, and by the time it's published, people will be reading books on Kindle. I have the world's worst timing. I'm a musician, and I did my last LP a few months before the first CDs came out, and albums became obsolete. Not long after I published my first book, Kindle came out, and people aren't buying books; they're downloading them. Now I'm getting ready to publish another book, and I'm making a CD, when CDs are losing their popularity. I can predict the future. If I decide to do something, it's on the verge of disappearing."

"Maybe you should help me pick a lottery number," Khristie said, laughing.

Brian and I laughed, and Khristie responded, "No, seriously, you should want me to win the lottery, because I'd use it to help other people. It's what I really want to do."

"That's good," Brian added. "I buy donuts at Dunkin' Doughnuts every couple of weeks and take them to the homeless shelter."

"Which one?" Khristie asked.

"The one here in Ansonia," Brian answered. "I take them to the battered women's shelter in Bridgeport too. I don't have a lot of money, and I have four kids, but I do what I can to help others. They really appreciate it."

I put my book down. God was writing on our hearts.

Khristie leaned over the counter, her eyes bright with enthusiasm. "If I won the lottery, the first thing I'd do is build a beautiful shelter for the homeless."

She had a faraway look in her eye, and I knew she could see the place of her dreams. "It would have beautiful grounds and buildings, and I'd take in all the homeless, and give them a place to live."

Brian said, "I'd really like to see that. We really need it."

"Are you talking about homeless people or homeless animals?" I asked Khristie.

"Both," she said. "I'd take in homeless animals and give homeless people jobs taking care of them, and they'd have a beautiful place to live."

"Boy, that really sounds good," Brian said. "I coach sports teams for the handicapped. I do whatever I can to help other people."

And the conversation flowed.

"My wife and I visit the sick and shut-in," I said. "Most of the time, we don't know the person we're visiting, but it doesn't make any difference to them. They're just happy to have visitors."

"That's right," Brian said. "When my dad was in the hospital a while back, I went up to see him, and there was someone visiting him I'd never seen before. 'Who's that?' I asked. 'I don't know,' my dad had said, 'he just came to see me.' "

Then I told them the story of Rose, the woman who shared a room with the mother of my wife's friend. They both seemed touched by the story.

"So, you're a writer," Khristie said. "What do you write about?"

"Moments like these," I said. "There's a beautiful story happening right now."

Then I told them the story about the ninety-year-old woman who waited on my wife and me at the Duchess restaurant, just three or four blocks away from the gas station.

By then business was picking up, and one of the mechanics came in and told Brian that his car was ready. When he got up, he turned and walked back to me with a warm smile on his face.

"My name's Brian," he said, sticking out his hand.

"Mine's Jerry," I said, reaching out to shake his hand. "It was real nice meeting you."

Sitting there by myself, I leaned back in the warm sunlight that was pouring through the big plate-glass windows. I thought of Khristie, who'd said that she just finished reading a book yesterday. She'd been sitting in the sunlight just as I was, and read for two hours, relaxing and enjoying the story. I sat there in the sunlight enjoying this one. As I sat there, I reached over to get my Bible. I'd been reading it starting in Genesis, with the intention of finally reading the whole book. I had a book marker in the place where I'd stopped reading, and when I opened the book to the marker, I had to smile.

Driving down to the gas station, I'd been thinking about a song my friend Jerry Rau wrote: "Driving in the Right-hand Lane." I always liked that song. It was about all the beautiful things you can see when you're driving leisurely in the right-hand lane. I wanted to refer to the song in another story I was working on, and the passage about the lilies of the field came to mind. I thought to myself, "I'll look up that passage in my concordance when I get home." That was why I smiled when I opened my Bible and read the first paragraph. My eye skimmed down to the verse that leapt off the page: "Consider the lilies how they grow. They do not labor or spin. Yet I tell you, not even Solomon in all his splendor was not dressed like one of these" (Luke 12:27 NIV).

Reading on, I came to a passage that fit our conversation in the Sunoco station:

> Do not be afraid, little flock; for your Father has been pleased to give you the kingdom. Sell your possessions, and give to the poor. Provide purses for yourselves that will not wear out, a treasure in heaven that will not be exhausted, where no thief comes near and no moth destroys. For where your treasure is, there your heart will be also.
>
> (Luke 12:32–34 NIV)

Reading these words of Jesus, I thought of Khristie, who was now off somewhere in a back room, and Brian, who was on his way home. I knew where their hearts lay.

When Khristie reappeared, she had my work order in hand, and I stepped up to the counter to pay the bill.

"I just have to read you something," I said, and I read the two scriptural passages from St. Luke. "I thought of you when I read the call to give to the poor," I said. "I don't believe in coincidences. I read these passages for a reason."

When I paid my bill, Khristie handed me my receipt and said, "This has been a hard day. As you can see, our gas pumps are down, and I was feeling pretty low, myself. I feel a lot better now."

And she left me with a warm smile, just as Brian had.

I'm not a Bible-toting Christian. I rarely walk around carrying a Bible, and I don't ever remember reading a passage from the Bible to someone I'd only just met. But I had my Bible for a reason, and I was led to the Scriptures because they spoke to the moment. If I'd gone with my original plan of going to get groceries while my car was being serviced, I would have missed a treasure. And that's where my heart lies.

THE GOSPEL IN BLACK AND WHITE

I grew up with Roy Rogers and Gene Autry. My buddies and I would meet them every Saturday at the Hitching Post, where they served a steady diet of cowboy movies. My friend Jim and I knew all about being cowboys, even though we were only eleven years old.

> Jim you take the left side, and I'll take the right
> My guns are ready-loaded and I'm itching to fight
> There'll be a few less hombres goin' to live to see tonight
> When we go down to the Hitching Post
>
> We'll meet Hopalong Cassidy and Lash Larue
> Roy and Gabby promised that they'd be there, too
> And when we get together, there's nothing we can't do
> When we get down to the Hitching Post[37]

In my neighborhood, the argument raged about who was better—Roy Rogers or Gene Autry. We even argued about whose horse was better—Trigger or Champion. Roy had the Sons of the Pioneers in his corner, but most of the guys hesitated being Roy Rogers for fear that one of the girls in the neighborhood would insist on being Dale Evans. One thing the singing cowboy movies had in common was their lack of realism. When Roy or Gene chased the villains on horseback, *they'd end up riding by the same rock outcrop two or three times. No matter how hard the fight, neither Roy nor Gene ever mussed a hair on their head, and their shirts never had a spot or wrinkle on them after the fight.*

> *Cowboys all were honest then, their horses all were trusty*
> *And when they slept out in the rain, their guns never got rusty*
> *And when they fought, they never lost,*
> *but they never won the girl*
> *And the buttons on the shirts they wore were simulated pearl*[38]

Hollywood has always been in the business of entertaining people. Realism was never a high priority. People had enough realism in their own lives. In the old cowboy movies, that worked fine. No one took them seriously. When people came to see movies about the life of Christ, they had higher expectations.

Most of us grew up with our perception of biblical characters shaped by the actors who portrayed them. When we read about Moses in the Bible, the image that comes to mind foremost is Charlton Heston. It's hard to imagine Moses looking like anyone else. But what if Moses actually looked more like Mickey Rooney? Can you imagine Mickey Rooney parting the Red Sea?

According to the Bible, Moses would never have been able to deliver his lines with the authority of Charlton Heston. Moses questioned God about whether he could speak eloquently enough so that people would believe him.

> And Moses said unto the Lord, O my Lord, I am not eloquent, neither, heretofore, not since thou hast spoken unto thy servant: but I am slow of speech, and of a slow tongue. . . . And the anger of the Lord was kindled against Moses, and he said, is not Aaron the Levite thy brother? I know that he can speak well. And also, behold, he cometh forth to meet thee: and when he seeth thee, he will be glad in his heart. And thou shalt speak unto him, and put words in his mouth: and I will be with thy mouth, and with his mouth, and teach thee what thou shalt say.
>
> (Exodus 4:10, 14–15)

The Gospel in Black and White

In *The Ten Commandments*, Moses spoke with great power and authority. Does anyone remember who played Aaron?

The actors who portrayed Jesus in movies were chosen for their ability to sell tickets at the box office, not because they looked anything like him. Did Jesus really look like Jeffrey Hunter, who portrayed him in the *King of Kings*? Jeffrey Hunter was blond, with incredible deep-blue eyes. If Jesus showed up for a casting call to play himself in a Hollywood movie, he probably wouldn't get the part.

Now don't get me wrong. Like everyone else, my faith was nurtured and strengthened through Hollywood movies. When I think of Moses, I see Charlton Heston parting the Red Sea, just like everyone else. Even though Jeffrey Hunter didn't look anything like Jesus, *King of Kings* was one of the better movies Hollywood made about the life of Christ, and I'm glad I saw it. But, the Bible is in black and white. It's not in widescreen Technicolor. Christ and the disciples wore simple homespun robes that got dirty and most likely looked the worse for wear. They spent most of their time walking down dirt roads, and if anything, they probably looked a little grubby.

The custom of washing people's feet was for practical reasons. If someone had been walking all day on a dirt road wearing sandals, their feet would be dirty by the end of the day. Christ took this practical task and used it to teach his disciples the importance of serving others.

> So after he had washed their feet, and had taken his garments, and was set down again, he said unto them, know ye what I have done? Ye call me Master and Lord; and ye say well; for so I am. If I then, your Lord and Master, have washed your feet; ye also ought to wash one another's feet. For I have given you an example, that ye should do as I have done to you. Verily I say unto you, The servant is not greater than his Lord; neither is he that is sent greater than he that sent him.
>
> (John 13:12–16)

The custom no longer makes sense in today's society, but the principle still holds true.

In 1964, Pier Paolo Pasolini, an Italian director, made a movie depicting the life of Christ called *The Gospel According to St. Matthew*. The film was in black and white. Many film critics consider it the best cinematic portrayal of the life of Christ ever made. Of all movie directors, Pasolini was probably the least likely to make a movie on the life of Christ. He was a Marxist atheist. It just goes to show: God uses whomever he chooses to do his work. Pasolini approached his story as if he were doing a documentary. Almost all the dialogue is taken directly from the gospel of Saint Matthew, and there are long stretches where there is no narrative to explain the scenes as they unfold. Pasolini used nonprofessionals as actors. The key role of Jesus was played by Enrique Irazoqui, a nineteen-year-old economics student from Spain. Enrique had an intensity about him unlike any I've ever seen in portrayals of Jesus. He spoke with great authority, delivering the memorable teachings of Christ in a way that demanded attention.

Pasolini was an Italian neorealist, and he brought a gritty, unglamorous perspective to Christ's ministry. None of the apostles were Hollywood handsome, and yet their ordinariness and rugged features made them more believable than smooth-faced Hollywood actors.

When the opening credits for the movie are rolling, an African choir sings an exuberant song. There are no swelling passages with a full orchestra. Pasolini's use of music was as eclectic as his choices of actors. Johann Sebastian Bach joins ranks with Wolfgang Amadeus Mozart and Sergei Prokofiev. The black folk-and-gospel singer Odetta welcomes the baby Jesus with "Sometimes I Feel Like a Motherless Child." When a crippled man approaches Jesus seeking to be healed, his tortured gait is balanced perfectly with Blind Willie Johnson's wordless bottleneck guitar playing "Dark Was the Night, Cold Was the Ground."

Why is it important to represent Christ as realistically as possible? When the angel of the Lord appeared to Joseph, he announced that Mary was to conceive a child through the Holy Spirit. The baby was to be named Jesus and would grow to be a man, but he was also God.

> Now the birth of Jesus Christ was on this wise: When as his mother Mary was espoused to Joseph, before they came together, she was found with child of the Holy Ghost . . . . Now all this was done, that it might be fulfilled which was spoken of the Lord by the prophet, saying: Behold a virgin shall be with child, and shall bring forth a son, and they shall call his name Immanuel, which being interpreted is, God, with us.
>
> (Matthew 1:18, 22–23)

In the final times of his ministry, the disciples were still unsure about Christ's divine nature. As often seemed to happen, it was Thomas who questioned Christ.

> Thomas saith unto him, Lord, we know not whither thou goest; and how can we know the way? Jesus saith unto him, I am the way, the truth and the life: no man cometh unto the Father, but by me. If ye had known me, ye should have known my Father also; and from henceforth ye know him, and have seen him. Then Philip questioned Jesus about God the father. Phillip saith unto him, Lord show us the Father, and it sufficeth us. Jesus saith unto him, Have I been so long time with you, and yet hast thou not known me, Philip? He that hath seen me hath seen the Father.
>
> (John 14:5–9)

Like the apostles Thomas and Philip, we long to see the Father. We don't have to look any further than his beloved Son, Jesus, to see him. Unlike Thomas and Philip, we are not blessed to see Jesus walking this earth. But there will come a time when we finally meet Jesus.

> *When I come to see Jesus, the man who set me free*
> *The one who lived and suffered, and died for you and me*
> *I'm going to thank him for all he brought me*
> *I'm going to thank him for what God taught me*
> *I'm going to thank him for the heavenly Bible,*
> *I'm going to thank him for the old time revival*
> *I'm going to thank him for the heavenly vision*
> *I'm going to thank him for the old time religion*

Then I'm going to sing, sing Hallelujah
And I'm going to shout, shout troubles over
And my soul looks back in wonder
How I got over, how I got over
How I got over[39]

When we get to glory, we will see Christ face-to-face, and we will know him as if we've known him all our lives.
Amen.

DANCING ON THE TOES OF HIS SHOES

Since the beginning of time, people have danced to express joy. Of all the dancers in the Bible, none could top King David for exuberance. When David brought the ark of the covenant into the city of David, his heart was filled with gladness and he danced for joy: "And David danced before the Lord with all his might" (2 Samuel 6:14).

Not everyone approved of his dancing, though.

> And as the ark of the Lord came into the city of David, Michal, Saul's daughter looked through a window and saw King David leaping and dancing before the Lord, and she despised him in her heart. (Verse 16)

> In his exuberance, David had experienced a wardrobe malfunction.

After David presented his offerings to the Lord, he returned to the home of Saul and reproached Michal. Then David returned to bless his household and Michal, the daughter of Saul came out to meet David, and said, "How glorious was the King of Israel today, who uncovered himself today in the eyes of the handmaidens of the servants, as one of the vain fellows shamelessly uncovereth himself." (Verse 20)

You can hear her voice dripping with sarcasm. Her criticism did not go unpunished.

And David said unto Michal, it was before the Lord, which chose me before thy father, and before all his house, to appoint me ruler over the people of the Lord, over Israel. Therefore will I play before the Lord. . . . Therefore, Michal the daughter of Saul had no children unto the day of her death. (Verses 21, 23)

Even Snoopy, in the comic strip Peanuts, *often danced for joy. As always, Lucy was very critical of Snoopy. Despite reminding him that the world is full of "doom, defeat, and despair," Snoopy refused to stop dancing. As Christians, nothing can separate us from the joy of Christ.*

And ye now therefore have sorrow; but I will see you again, and your heart shall rejoice, and your joy no man taketh from you.
(John 16:22)

Shall we dance?

After all these years, the memory still remains of watching a father dancing with his young daughter while she was standing on the toes of his shoes. I can see the look of love between them as he supported her gently, her arms clasped tightly around his waist. I don't remember who the man or the little girl was, or where they were dancing, but I remember the memory. It's not one you'd forget. That memory comes back so strongly, because I picture my brother-in-law Everette dancing with his wife, Bootsy, when she could no longer support her body. He held her gently but firmly, and they danced around the room of their home in Brooklyn, with her standing on the toes of his shoes.

It hadn't always been that way.

It all began on Green Avenue, in Brooklyn, where Everette and Bootsy first met as teenagers when Bootsy's family moved into the brownstone next door. Not long after that, Everette enlisted in the army as a paratrooper in the 82nd Army Airborne Division. He was just eighteen years old. Three years later when he was discharged from the army, he came back home to Green Avenue. There was a new sound on the street as kids throughout New York were gathering under streetlamps, working on their harmonies. Green Avenue was no exception. Everette's friend, Harry James, who lived across the street, had formed a rhythm-and-blues group with three of his buddies. They called themselves the Rays. A small record company in New York recorded one of their songs, "Silhouettes," and it went to number three on the pop charts. I have never been to Brooklyn, but I sang those same songs on the streets of my hometown in southern Wisconsin.

> *It wasn't all that long ago*
> *When we listened to the radio*
> *We all knew the songs by heart*
> *And everybody sang their part*
>
> *And every corner had a group*
> *We sang "Searchin'" and "Alley Oop"*
> *And even though those days are gone*
> *I still like to sing those songs*[40]

Love was in the air, and Everette and Bootsy saw each other in a new light. It all started out simply enough. They'd always loved music and they both loved to dance, and it wasn't long before they started hitting all the jazz clubs in the city. They'd take the A train up to Harlem, and to Minton's, where the top jazz musicians of the day hung out after hours, or drop by Small's Paradise. If they wanted to go dancing, the Savoy Ballroom was the place to go. Further downtown just north of Fifty-Second Street, Charlie Parker held court at Birdland—the club that was named in his honor. All the jazz greats played Birdland at one time or another, and Everette and Bootsy heard most of them, from The Prez (Lester Young) and Coleman Hawkins, to Dizzy Gillespie, Charlie Christian, and Thelonius Monk. When they weren't dancing in the clubs, Everette and Bootsy danced to the new rhythm-and-blues songs on the radio. They'd slow dance to Johnny Ace's "Pledging My Love," the Moonglows' "Sincerely," and the Penguins's "Earth Angel." Georgia Gibbs took Etta James's R & B hit, "Roll with Me, Henry," changed the lyrics, and had a hit with "Dance with Me, Henry." She knew the way to a man's heart was to get him on the dance floor. Everette never turned down a chance to dance with Bootsy. And as the Five Satins sang, each dance drew them closer to the aisle.

In 1956, Everette and Bootsy walked down that aisle and pledged their love for each other. For many years, all was well with them, and they let the good times roll. Everette had a steady job as manager of a hotel-and-restaurant-supply company, and they found a place to live in Brooklyn. In the summer, they vacationed in the islands, and they were blessed with two children. Life was good.

The time finally came when Everette and Bootsy's lives were transformed forever. Bootsy went in for her annual checkup, and the doctor informed her that she was diabetic. It shouldn't have been a surprise because her family had a history of diabetes. She took the news in stride. She and Everette knew that their love would carry them through.

> *Through the good times and bad times, fair weather and foul*
> *There is nothing as strong as a bond of the heart*[41]

As the years passed, a succession of strokes slowly robbed Bootsy of her vitality and strength. She could no longer walk and needed constant care, and Everette retired so he could stay home and take care of her. Bootsy's dancing days were over, but her love of music was just as strong. She spent her days writing songs, and when Everette would play the old records, she'd wave her arms in the air or clap to the rhythm, sitting in her wheelchair.

The first time I visited Everette and Bootsy, Bootsy was in bed. He gently lifted her into her wheelchair and wheeled her out to the living room, where my wife, Ruth (Everette's sister), and his brother Irving and sister-in-law Sarah were waiting. It was a joyous time, and even though Bootsy couldn't join in on the conversation, I could see how much she enjoyed being with the family. I had talked with Everette about my love of the old rhythm-and-blues songs, and when I got back home, I copied a cassette of my favorite songs from the 'fifties.

The next time I spoke with Everette, he told me how excited Bootsy was, hearing all the old songs. They brought back such wonderful memories.

*And sometimes the memories came back with a song
Just as surely as if she was there*[42]

When Bootsy felt the desire to dance, she'd call Everette and say, "Honey, will you dance with me?" Everette would carefully lift her out of her wheelchair and rest her feet on the toes of his shoes. Bootsy would wrap her arms around his neck while he held her gently but firmly around her waist, and they'd slow dance around the room to the old songs: "Only You," "My Prayer," and "In the Still of the Night"—songs they'd danced to so many years ago on those lazy summer nights on Green Avenue.

*Where are the men who can find their contentment
In a living room waltz, or a walk by the sea?
Who still know the meaning of now and forever
And a love that can last you through eternity?*[43]

Bootsy may never have had diamonds on the soles of her shoes like the young woman Paul Simon sang about, but she had a loving man who could find his contentment dancing with her in their living room with her resting her feet on the toes of his shoes. All she needed to do was wave her arms in rhythm to the music and say to him, "Dance with me, Everette."

THE SHEPHERD'S WATCH: THE SONG

The Shepherd's Watch
Words and music by Jerry Rasmussen
©Copyright 2010

The darkness closes around you
Storm clouds fill the sky
You lie on your bed and you wonder
If you call out, who'll hear you cry?

CHORUS:

Don't be afraid, put your trust in him
Though you walk through the valley of the shadow of death
For Christ knows his sheep, and if you know him
No harm will befall you on the Shepherd's watch
He'll lay you down in green pastures
By the waters so still and deep
You'll feel a peace down in your soul
Knowing you're in the Shepherd's keep

His rod and his staff they give comfort
To those who've lost their way
For Christ will leave the ninety nine
Just for one who has gone astray

Whenever anyone asks, "What is the most popular song of all time?" the answer is usually "White Christmas." When it comes to record sales, that's certainly the right answer. The *Guinness Book of World Records,* 2009 edition, lists the song as a 100-million seller. The 23rd Psalm never hit the top forty, but it's most certainly the most popular song of all time. We don't think of the Psalms as songs anymore, but that's what they were originally written to be. It could easily be claimed that King David was the greatest singer/songwriter of all time. Forget Lennon and McCartney. There's something about the imagery of the 23rd Psalm that gives us great comfort. That's why the psalm is so often recited at funerals.

When I wrote this song, I made no attempt to put the 23rd Psalm into a song, as has so often been done with the Lord's Prayer. But make no mistake, the imagery is woven throughout the song. I pray the comfort is, too.

JERRY'S MUSIC

Jerry began performing at the Gaslight Café in Greenwich Village in the early '60s, when Bob Dylan, Dave Van Ronk, Peter, Paul, and Mary, and Richie Havens were starting their careers. He has shared the stage with Pete Seeger, The Highwaymen, and performed in the first Hootenanny at Town Hall in New York City. He has been compared to Garrison Keillor, and his songs have been featured on Prairie Home Companion. Jerry has performed in concerts and folk festivals from Massachusetts to Missouri, and did a concert for PBS as part of the In the Tradition series. His songs have appeared in folk journals and magazines, including *Sing Out!* magazine, and the *Songbook of New Folk Favorites*, published by Hal Leonard. Jerry's songs have been recorded by more than twenty other artists.

Discography
Get Down Home – Folk Legacy Records CD77
The Secret Life of Jerry Rasmussen – Folk Legacy Records CD101
Handful of Songs – Jack Rabbit 01
Without That Night – The Gospel Messengers – Jackrabbit 2
Back When I Was Young –Jackrabbit 3
Lord Send Me – Jackrabbit 4
Gospel Nights – Jackrabbit 5

Many of the songs in this book can be heard at https:/soundcloud.com/jerryrasmussen tracks

His CDs can be purchased through www.cdbaby.com, or from Jerry's website at www.razzgospel/com

Contact:
Jerry Rasmussen
94 Hillcrest Ave.
Derby, CT 06418
geraldrasmussen@SBCglobal.net

ENDNOTES

1. "Find Rest Tonight" – words and music by Jerry Rasmussen
2. "Last Chance for Salvation" – words and music by Jerry Rasmussen
3. "Jesus Loves the Little Children" – C. Herbert Woolston
4. "Jesus Loves Me" – traditional
5. "You Know You're Getting Old" – Jerry Rasmussen
6. "The Shepherd's Watch" – words and music by Jerry Rasmussen
7. "Jesus Loves Me" – William B. Bradbury
8. "Speak for Jesus" – traditional
9. Traditional
10. "Blind Barnabus" – traditional
11. Matthew 18:20
12. "The Carpenter's Son" – words and music by Jerry Rasmussen
13. *Merriam-Webster's Collegiate Dictionary*
14. "Ships on the Prairie" – words and music by Jerry Rasmussen
15. "Paradise Found" – words and music by Jerry Rasmussen
16. "Paradise Found"
17. "Paradise Found"
18. "Paradise Found"

19. "Paradise Found"
20. "Hold On" – traditional
21. "Find Rest Tonight" – words and music by Jerry Rasmussen
22. "Farther Along" – W. B. Stevens
23. "Never Alone" – traditional
24. "Joy to the World" – words by Isaac Watts
25. "His Eye Is on the Sparrow" –words and music by Charles H. Gabriel
26. "He's Working on Me" – words and music by Jerry Rasmussen
27. "Little Black Train" – traditional
28. "Back When I Was Young" – words and music by Jerry Rasmussen
29. "Just Because You Like to Do It, That Don't Make It Right"
30. "Farther Along" – W.B. Stevens
31. "Smile" – Charlie Chaplin
32. "Stop for a Minute" – words and music by Jerry Rasmussen
33. "Three Speeds Forward and No Speeds Back" – words and music by Jerry Rasmussen
34. "When I Get Home – C. Austin Miles
35. "Drowning in the Details of Life" – words and music by Jerry Rasmussen
36. "Only Believe" – traditional
37. "The Hitching Post" – words and music by Jerry Rasmussen
38. "Back When I Was Young" – words and music by Jerry Rasmussen
39. "How I Got Over" – C. H. Cobbs
40. "Ten Pound Radio" – words and music by Jerry Rasmussen
41. "Bond of the Heart" – words and music by Jerry Rasmussen
42. "Tortoise Shell Comb" – words and music by Jerry Rasmussen
43. "Lavender Ladies" – words and music by Jerry Rasmussen

CONTACT INFORMATION

REDEMPTION PRESS

To order additional copies of this book, please visit
www.redemption-press.com.
Also available on Amazon.com and BarnesandNoble.com
Or by calling toll free 1 (844) 273-3336.